The Assassination
of John F. Kennedy

The Assassination of John F. Kennedy

AN ANNOTATED FILM, TV, AND VIDEOGRAPHY, 1963–1992

Compiled by
Anthony Frewin

FOREWORD BY MARTIN SHORT

Bibliographies and Indexes
in Mass Media and Communications, Number 8

GREENWOOD PRESS
Westport, Connecticut • London

Library of Congress Cataloging-in-Publication Data

Frewin, Anthony.
   The assassination of John F. Kennedy : an annotated film, TV, and
videography, 1963-1992 / compiled by Anthony Frewin ; foreword by
Martin Short.
      p. cm. — (Bibliographies and indexes in mass media and
communications, ISSN 1041-8350 ; no. 8)
   Includes bibliographical references (p.) and indexes.
   ISBN 0-313-28982-4 (alk. paper)
   1. Kennedy, John F. (John Fitzgerald), 1917-1963 — Assassination —
Film catalogs.   2. Kennedy, John F. (John Fitzgerald), 1917-1963 —
Assassination — Video catalogs.   I. Title.   II. Series.
E842.9.F73   1993
364.1'524 — dc20   93-24763

British Library Cataloguing in Publication Data is available.

Library of Congress Catalog Card Number: 93-24763
ISBN: 0-313-28982-4
ISSN: 1041-8350

First published in 1993

Greenwood Press, 88 Post Road West, Westport, CT 06881
An imprint of Greenwood Publishing Group, Inc.

Printed in the United States of America

∞™

The paper used in this book complies with the
Permanent Paper Standard issued by the National
Information Standards Organization (Z39.48-1984).

10 9 8 7 6 5 4 3 2 1

Government, today, has grown
too strong to be safe. There
are no longer any citizens
in the world; there are only
subjects.

H. L. Mencken (1925)

Contents

Foreword

With this painstaking yet sharp and witty work Anthony Frewin has filled a long-felt gap in John F. Kennedy assassination studies. Television (and film) is now the main source of most people's knowledge of contemporary history. For many it is the *only* source. This is especially true of the assassination of President Kennedy which was reported primarily on television when it happened and which has since scorched its way via television into our collective unconscious, most vividly through repeated broadcasts of those few blurred frames from Abraham Zapruder's 8mm home movie.

In Britain much of the most striking JFK assassination research has first been revealed or popularized not in books, but on television: starting in 1967 with Mark Lane's then shocking assertions of a cover-up by the Warren Commission, through various BBC documentaries, London Weekend Television's five-hour *The Trial of Lee Harvey Oswald* (1988), and Nigel Turner's spectacular but deeply flawed *The Men Who Killed Kennedy* (1988 and 1991). In America there was the additional drama of the stream of testimony given in the 1978 House Select Committee on Assassinations broadcasts by PBS.

Television producers, researchers and reporters have themselves dug up a large amount of the truth about JFK's assassination, by seeking out and interviewing a vast number of witnesses which neither the FBI, other state agencies or distinguished authors have found, or even tried to find. You can write a book without ever consulting an original source but, when making a television documentary, if you haven't got a stack of firsthand, preferably 'new,' witnesses, you don't have a show.

Frewin's labour of love (and scholarship) won't recoup his expenses in producing it, but future scholars, JFK assassination buffs, television producers and documentary film-makers will be deeply grateful to him. This filmography is everything a filmography should be, and more.

Martin Short

London

March, 1993

[Martin Short produced, wrote and narrated *Crime Inc.*, the highly acclaimed 1984 Thames TV series on the Mafia and organised crime in America. He has written several books and has recently produced a major TV documentary on the assassination of the Italian Prime Minister Aldo Morro.]

Introduction

President John F. Kennedy was assassinated at 12:30pm Central Standard Time on Friday, 22 November 1963, in Dealey Plaza, Dallas. At 1:00pm CST he was declared dead at Parkland Hospital. Fifty minutes later, in another part of Dallas, Lee Harvey Oswald was arrested at the Texas Theater on Jefferson Blvd. Within hours Oswald was presented to the world as the assassin and portrayed as a lone, mad left-winger. Two days later, on Sunday, 24 November, Oswald was shot and killed in the basement of the Dallas Police Department by the operator of a local striptease joint, Jack Ruby. The slaying took place in front of reporters and news cameramen and was broadcast live on US television.

On 29 November 1963 President Lyndon B. Johnson appointed a seven-member Commission under Earl Warren to investigate the assassination. Nearly a year later, on 27 September 1964, the Warren Commission released its *Report*. Warren's conclusions merely echoed the line that had been leached out to trusty journalists within hours of the assassination: Oswald was a lone, mad, left-winger without accomplices or associates. There the matter should have rested. But it didn't. Even before Earl Warren delivered his *Report* to Johnson writers, journalists and students of the assassination were registering disquiet at the official Washington line. Why was some evidence ignored? Why were some questions left unanswered? Why were contradictions left unresolved? Why were holes in the case against Lee Harvey Oswald smoothed over or ignored? Why was information being withheld? *What* was being withheld?

Starting with a couple of lone, isolated voices in 1964 the number of 'critics' (of the Warren *Report*) grew steadily each year until by the late 1960s one could speak of a 'critical community' of sizeable dimensions. Articles, pamphlets, and books were published in increasing numbers questioning the lone mad assassin theory, the 'magic bullet' and other aspects of the slaying of Jack Kennedy as 'explained' by the *Report*. Earl Warren's findings were soon largely discredited and, as we now know, there is no evidence at all that can put a rifle in Lee Harvey Oswald's hands on the 22 November 1963.

Daily, almost, the critical literature grew...and grew and grew. It was difficult trying to keep up with it until in 1980 DeLloyd J. Guth, a specialist in pre-Reformation legal history, and David R. Wrone, a professor at the University of Wisconsin, published a full-scale bibliography on the literature engendered by the events of 22 November: *The Assassination of John F. Kennedy: A Comprehensive Historical and Legal Bibliography, 1963-1979* (Westport, Connecticut: Greenwood Press). The work runs to over 5000 entries, including newspaper articles, and is essential for any serious student of the assassination. Amongst the sections in Guth and Wrone, as I shall refer to the work hereinafter, are a couple of rudimentary listings of films and TV programs.

As the 1980s wore on more TV programs and documentaries were produced. It became apparent that someone should keep track of them. Unlike books, TV programs and films are soon forgotten or overlooked, and yet here was a growing body of important evidence that was going down the chute to oblivion (or near oblivion). Let me give you one telling example of what we were losing. There are dozens of important witnesses who have never written a word yet have been interviewed on camera, witnesses like Jim Leavelle (handcuffed to Oswald when Ruby shot him) and Earlene Roberts (Oswald's landlady). Who was keeping tabs on this?

The present filmography started life as what I thought would be a six-page article (well, perhaps a few pages more) for *Lobster* magazine bringing Guth and Wrone's film and TV listings up to date and adding brief annotation lacking in their work. A checklist in other words. The article slowly increased in length and what I thought originally would have been completed in a few weekends expanded to several years. Finally a circle had to be drawn around an imperfect work. *Sic transit.* Nobody will be more aware of its failings and shortcomings than the compiler.

The subject areas of this filmography may readily be gleaned from the contents page.

The greater part of the entries described here are from North America. England is well-represented also, but only a few items come from other countries.

Chapter 1 lists newsreel footage of Oswald in New Orleans. Chapters 2, 3 and 4 list all film and tape of Dealey Plaza and its immediate aftermath.

Chapter 5, 'Documentary Films, TV Programs, Videos,' details in chronological order the major and most relevant productions dealing principally with the assassination of JFK. Here I have avoided the Kennedy 'hagiographical' and 'remembrance' programs unless there is something new or important in them relating to the assassination. Here I have also ignored the whole burgeoning sub-genre of JFK material relating to the Mob, personal and political scandals,

Marilyn Monroe and so on, a sub-genre only of peripheral interest. Again I have made exceptions where there is something new or important.

Chapter 6 lists compilation videos put out by Collector's Archives in Canada, while chapter 7 lists two commercially made films that Oswald is alleged to have watched with Marina, together with the two playing at the Texas Theater in Dallas when he was arrested.

Chapter 8, 'Theatrical Motion Pictures,' lists in chronological order commercial films that were either inspired by the assassination, have some connection with it, or contain more than passing allusions.

The remaining chapters are self-explanatory. Chapters 10 and 11 will be useful for anyone wishing to pursue their own research into films and tapes relating to the subject.

The chronological arrangement of, principally, chapter 5, the largest section of the book should be described further. An entry with a day, a month and a year of production (or broadcast or release) presents no problems. Where the year and the month are given, but no day, I have pushed the item to the end of that month and if other semi-orphans are to be found there I have arranged them alphabetically under title. The same arrangement applies to an entry that has a year only (no day or month), to the end of that year and then alphabetised.

I hope that the general arrangement of the book into the 12 chapters together with the cross references, appendix and indexes, supplies enough navigational aids for the reader to find what he or she is looking for without going hopelessly adrift. The arrangement has been devised to make this guide easily accessible to readers with different interests and research needs.

A work such as this cannot be a primer on the subject so I have assumed in the reader a working knowledge of the assassination. However, I have made the present volume as self-explanatory and contained as I could without it reading like an elementary text-book. I have also eschewed the use of abbreviations except for a handful too well known to be spelt out: if you don't know what CIA or FBI stands for you may be wasting your time in this neck of the woods. TSBD is used frequently and refers to the Texas School Book Depository on Elm Street at Dealey Plaza. B&W means a film or video is in black-and-white; without this designation assume the production under discussion is in color. PD means Police Department.

The terms 'research community' and 'critical community' refer to those who disagree with some or all of the findings of the Warren Commission and other government investigations into the assassination. A 'critic' means a member of those communities.

None of the films or videos should be too hard to find as the critical community is heavily populated with collectors and hoarders. No item should be beyond a persistent searcher. A good first port-of-call is the JFK Assassination Information Center, West End Market Place, 603 Munger #310, Box 40, Dallas, TX 75202, USA (tel: (214) 871.2770), and if you write do not forget to include a stamped, addressed envelope or International Reply coupons. The Collector's Archives in Canada is also worth trying, but this is a commercially-run enterprise and often expensive. The address is given at the beginning of chapter 6.

Articles aside, there are only two good books on the photographic evidence in the JFK assassination. Josiah Thompson's *Six Seconds in Dallas* (1967) is still a fundamentally important study of Dealey Plaza utilizing the evidence of still photos and movie footage, though some of his conclusions have been called into question. The other work is Harold Weisberg's *Photographic Whitewash* (1967, 1976), but here the concern is not so much cataloging and analysing the photographic evidence as charting the investigative agencies negligence (and uninterest) in handling it.

In 1965, one hundred years after Abraham Lincoln was assassinated, Harper & Row in New York published the Kunhardts' magisterial *Twenty Days: A Narrative in Text and Pictures of the Assassination of Abraham Lincoln and the Twenty Days and Nights That Followed - The Nation in Mourning, The Long Trip Home to Springfield*. The work contains over 300 illustrations (every known contemporary photograph and important picture) taken from the collection built up over a lifetime by Frederick Hill Meserve (1865-1962).

Difficult as it is to believe, but among the hundreds of books published on the JFK assassination there is still no work equivalent to the Kunhardts' Lincoln collection. I hope this filmography will re-focus the critical community's attention on the photographic evidence, both still and movie, and spur someone to undertake the task. It would be a great pity if we have to wait 100 years, until 2063, for such a study.

There are bound to be errors and omissions in the present book. I warmly welcome any comments, corrections and suggestions. These can be sent to me care of the publisher.

It seems customary today for writers to mention the soft- and hardware they have used to conjure their work into existence. I started by using Volkswriter/Total Word on a Hewlett Packard Vectra 386 and then when Volkswriter went out of business (and print drivers were no longer available) I switched to Word for Windows and purloined my son's Cruz 486SX (it had a better monitor). The book was printed out on a HP Laserjet.

Finally, it gives me much pleasure to discharge some thank-yous. It would be invidious and essentially unfair to single out any person for special mention in the acknowledgements. I owe a very great debt of thanks to all of the following: Martin Cannon, Amanda Collins, Geoffrey Crawley, Michael Eddowes, Dennis Lee Effle, Tim Everett, Mark Frewin, Nick Frewin, Mysha Frost, Robert E. Groden, Maria Harlan, Toni Hayward, Margaret Hennessey, Jim Houghan, Robert Johnson, Gary Mack, Mark Oakes, Robin Ramsay, Mike Royden, Anthony Sadleir, Dr. Cliff Scheiner, Martin Short, Steve Southgate, Angela Steger, Anthony Summers, Alan Tidswell, Judy Tobey, Lesley Walker, Harold Weisberg, Peter West, Kevin Wheeler, and Jack White.

Thanks also to Mildred Vasan of Greenwood Press for readily responding to the proposal for this book.

Anthony Frewin

St. Albans

March, 1993

The Assassination
of John F. Kennedy

1

Lee Harvey Oswald in New Orleans

Listed in chronological order.

[1] DOYLE, JAMES PATRICK.
Movie footage taken by a teenage boy who was on holiday with his family. Shot on 9 August 1963 in Canal Street showing Oswald (and associate/s?) distributing pro-Castro handbills.

This evidence was known to the FBI but not passed on to the Warren Commission.

The Doyle film was 'borrrowed' by the FBI for examination and later returned with many frames missing. Further, it was not the original that was returned to Doyle but a copy on a different film base. This copy blurred the edges of the frames and rendered identification of Oswald's associate/s difficult if not impossible.

What seems to be a brief clip is included in Dan Rather's *48 Hours* documentary, No. 169.

See Weisberg, *Oswald in New Orleans: Case for Conspiracy with the CIA* (1967), p316, and Weisberg v. the FBI, Civil Action No. 78-420, detailed by Guth and Wrone (below) at No. 181.

Guth and Wrone, *The Assassination of John F. Kennedy: A Comprehensive Historical and Legal Bibliography 1963-1979* (1980), No. 189.

[2] MARTIN, JACK.
Movie footage taken by a tourist of Oswald's 9 August 1963 handbill operation.
Known to the FBI but not given to the Warren Commission.
Guth and Wrone No. 190.

[3] WDSU-TV (1).
12 August 1963 - Oswald's appearance outside the Municipal Court of New Orleans filmed by a local TV station.

Oswald was fined $10 for the 9 August fracas.

WDSU was the local New Orleans affiliate of NBC. The station was owned by Edith and Edgar Stern. Mrs Stern was the daughter of Julius Rosenwald, one of the founders of Sears, Roebuck and Company. The Sterns were close friends of Clay Shaw and did much to support him after the Garrison indictment.

Guth and Wrone No. 191.

[4] WDSU-TV (2).
Oswald in front of the New Orleans Trade Mart on 16 August 1963 distributing pro-Castro leaflets.

In the film a white-haired man resembling Clay Shaw can be seen walking in front of the building towards Oswald, but then he turns and enters the Trade Mart. Oswald stops leafleting and heads in the man's direction. Jim Garrison and others believe the white-haired figure is Clay Shaw, but the film is inconclusive. This scene is re-created in Oliver Stone's *JFK*, No. 225.

The film was shot by Johann Rush, an employee of the TV station, who subsequently surfaced in the debate surrounding the Easterling allegations in Henry Hurt's *Reasonable Doubt* (1985). See 'News from Round the League' in *The Third Decade*, July 1986.

This footage is included in *Four Days in November*, No. 75, *The Day the Dream Died*, No. 147, *Ruby and Oswald*, No. 119, *The Men Who Killed Kennedy*, No. 167, Dan Rather's *48 Hours* documentary, No. 169, and *The JFK Assassination: The Jim Garrison Tapes*, No. 174.

Guth and Wrone No. 192.

[5] WWL-TV.
On 16 August 1963 cameraman Bob Jones filmed Oswald and another person distributing leaflets in front of the Trade Mart.

Included in David Wolper's documentary, *Four Days in November*, No. 75, *The Men Who Killed Kennedy*, No. 167, *48 Hours*, No. 169, *The JFK Assassination: The Jim Garrison Tapes*, No. 174, and *Assassination!*, No. 176.

Guth and Wrone No. 194.

[6] WDSU-TV (3).
A filmed interview with sound made by the station on 21 August 1963 with Oswald after he had been on a radio program, William Stuckey's *Latin Listening Post* (an audio tape can be obtained from the National Archives).

Included wholly or in part in *The Trial of Lee Harvey Oswald*, No. 138, *The Day the Dream Died*, No. 147, and also Nos. 167, 169 and 174.

Guth and Wrone No. 193.

2

Dealey Plaza

Listed in alphabetical order under the name of the photographer.

Clips from many of the films detailed below are included in *The Kennedy Assassination Photo Chronology* put out by Collector's Archives in Canada. The *Chronology* is concerned primarily with the stills taken on 22 November and uses movie clips merely for continuity: No. 161, below.

The best movie compilation is still Dallas Cinema Associates' *President Kennedy's Last Hour,* No. 35, though this does not include the Nix, Zapruder or Muchmore films.

A chart showing 'twenty-two photographers in Dealey Plaza and where they stood' is given on p12 of Josiah Thompson's *Six Seconds in Dallas* (1967). This is an essential help in understanding the photographic evidence (the chart also includes still photographers).

Beverly Oliver's lost film is noted in a later chapter at No. 241.

[7] ALLEN, RICHARD (DICK).
Amateur footage incorporated into *President Kennedy's Last Hour,* No. 35.
   Guth and Wrone No. 195

[8] ALYEA, THOMAS P.
A WFAA-TV cameraman who soon after the assassination ran towards the TSBD with his 16mm Bell & Howell 70DR camera, filming as he ran.
   Inside the TSBD Alyea shot five reels of film as the police searched the interior. This footage covered the discovery of the sniper's nest and the alleged assassination rifle. It seems that Alyea was the only cameraman in the TSBD at the time.
   The FBI were uninterested in acquiring the 500ft of film until many weeks

later when the footage had been edited down to a single composite reel and its evidentiary value impaired.

Several shots still exist and have been used in subsequent documentaries.

An FBI statement taken from Alyea and dated 3/27/64 is reproduced in Weisberg's *Photographic Whitewash* (1976), pps274-5. See also pps121-3 therein.

Guth and Wrone No. 198.

[9] BELL, F. M.
8mm color footage filmed from the south side of Main at the Houston junction.

Josiah Thompson interviewed Bell and reproduces frames from the film in *Six Seconds in Dallas* (1967).

Guth and Wrone No. 202.

[10] BENNEL, ALBERT.
A Dallas amateur who shot footage of the motorcade. He was a friend of Ernest Mantesana (see below) and like him was a member of the Dallas 8mm Movie Club (Cinema Guild of Texas).

See the FBI memo dated 4/28/64 in Weisberg's *Photographic Whitewash* (1976), p242.

Guth and Wrone No. 203.

[11] BOREN, BRYANT.
Amateur footage incorporated into *President Kennedy's Last Hour*, No. 35.

Guth and Wrone No. 206.

[12] BRENK, RUDOLF VIKTOR.
Brenk shot some six feet of 8mm Dynachrome color film of the motorcade with his Camex camera from the north-west corner of Harwood and Ross.

This amateur footage was incorporated into *President Kennedy's Last Hour*, No. 35, a documentary edited and produced by Brenk using amateur film shot by other members of the Dallas 8mm Club of which he was a member.

Guth and Wrone No. 208.

[13] BRONSON, CHARLES L.
Amateur's 8mm color footage of the assassination scene that was not discovered by critics until 1978.

In 1963 the film was viewed by the FBI who dismissed its importance. It then remained with Bronson until 1978 when the *Dallas Morning News* broke the story of its existence.

Bronson's film was shot some six minutes before the assassination and includes the sixth floor of the TSBD. Robert Groden examined the film and concluded that it showed the movement of two men in the sixth floor window and also movement by another figure in the arched window to the left who may or may not be one of the two figures. Some researchers believe this is the same movement captured in the Hughes film, No. 23. Hughes was standing only a few feet east of Bronson.

Bronson's film also shows the arrival of the ambulance to collect Jerry Belknap, a 23-year-old newspaper employee, who shortly before had suffered an 'epileptic seizure' on the west side of Houston. It has been suggested by Jerry D. Rose that Belknap's behaviour may have been a 'diversionary action to allow the assassins to move undetected into their assigned positions.'

As of September 1992 the Dallas offfice of the FBI is pressing for an independent scientific examination of the film.

A full analysis of the Bronson film is one of the six recommendations made by Carl Oglesby for furthering the JFK investigation in his *The JFK Assassination* (1992).

See also Groden and Livingstone's *High Treason* (1989), pps195-6, and earlier, *Dallas Morning News,* 26 November 1978, and the *New York Times*, 28 November 1978.

Rose's article discussing the Belknap seizure is in *The Third Decade*, November 1985, 'Dallas Police: The Manufacture of Confusion.'

The sharpest print I have seen of the film is included in *The JFK Assassination: The Jim Garrison Tapes*, No. 174.

Guth and Wrone No. 209.

[14] BROWN, JOE.
Amateur footage incorporated into *President Kennedy's Last Hour,* No. 35.
Not in Guth and Wrone.

[15] COOK, DONALD.
A KTTV-TV photographer listed by Richard Sprague but unverifiable. Still or motion picture?
See Sprague in References below.
Guth and Wrone No. 215.

[16] COUCH, MALCOLM.
An ABC-TV cameraman in the motorcade who filmed Dealey Plaza immediately after the assassination, including shots of the front of the TSBD. A. J. L'Hoste, No. 27, was another cameraman who worked with him. Couch was in the same car as David Weigman, No. 47.

Couch, incidentally, was called before the Warren Commission and said that Wes Wise 'who works for KRLD' saw Jack Ruby by the TSBD immediately after the assassination. Counsel dismissed this as hearsay. Corroboration for Ruby's presence in Dealey Plaza had also come from Jean Hill and Victoria Adams. The Commission never looked into the matter.

See Weisberg's *Photographic Whitewash* (1976), pps53-8.
   Guth and Wrone No. 216.
[17] DANIEL, JACK.
Amateur 8mm color footage discovered in 1978. The 10 second movie shows
events immediately after the assassination.
   Guth and Wrone No. 218.

[18] DARNELL, JAMES.
A WBAP-TV cameraman listed by Richard Sprague but unverifiable.
   See Sprague in References below.
   Guth and Wrone No. 219.

[19] DARROUZET, CHRIS.
An amateur's film of the motorcade that remained unknown and in private
possession until it was shown on ABC-TV's *Good Morning, America* program
on 22 November 1983, No. 129. Darrouzet filmed the motorcade just before it
reached Dealey Plaza.
   Not in Guth and Wrone.

[20] DORMAN, MRS. ELSIE T.
Color footage shot by an amateur from the fourth floor of the TSBD showing the
motorcade and the assassination. Dorman worked for the Scott-Foresman Co.
which had space in the TSBD.
   Dorman made a statement to the Secret Service but the film was neither
examined nor acquired by the FBI or the Warren Commission.
   With Dorman were three co-workers, one of whom, Victoria Adams, told the
FBI: 'we heard a shot, and there was a pause, and then a second shot, and then a
third shot. It sounded like a firecracker or a cannon at a football game, it seems
as if it came from the right below [the Grassy Knoll area] rather than from the
left above [the sixth floor window].'
   See Weisberg, *Photographic Whitewash* (1976), pps49-52.
   Guth and Wrone No. 222.

[21] GEWERTZ, MRS. IRVING.
Amateur footage incorporated into *President Kennedy's Last Hour*, No. 35.
   Guth and Wrone No. 224.

[22] GRAY, W. C.
Amateur footage incorporated into *President Kennedy's Last Hour*, No. 35.
   Guth and Wrone No. 225.

[23] HUGHES, ROBERT J.
Color footage by an amateur standing on the south-east corner of Main and

Houston who shot the motorcade proceeding east on Main Street, north on Houston Street and left on Elm Street directly in front of the TSBD.

Frames show what appears to be two moving figures in the window adjacent to the sniper's window in the TSBD while the sniper's window itself is empty (compare with the Bronson film, No. 13. Bronson was standing only a few feet west of Hughes). In 1975 CBS asked the Itek Corporation to examine the film and, perhaps predictably, Itek reported back that it could find no evidence of movement, a conclusion hotly disputed by the critical community.

Misrepresented in the FBI's five volume report to the Warren Commission, *Investigation of Assassination of President John F. Kennedy* (1963).

Clips are included in many documentary compilations, but for a full showing see *The Trial of Lee Harvey Oswald*, No. 138, and also *The Men Who Killed Kennedy*, No. 142. Probably the clearest print is that used in *The JFK Assassination: The Jim Garrison Tapes*, No. 174.

Hughes released the film himself in Dallas in 1963, No. 69 below.

A good account of Hughes and the Warren Commission's investigation is in Weisberg's *Photographic Whitewash* (1976), pps125-33. See also Anthony Summers' *The Kennedy Conspiracy* (1989), pps44-5. Josiah Thompson in *Six Seconds in Dallas* (1967) analyses and discusses the film in detail and reproduces several frames.

Guth and Wrone No. 227.

[24] JAMISON, J.
WBAT-TV cameraman who shot b&w footage, noted by Weisberg in *Photographic Whitewash* (1976).

Guth and Wrone No. 229.

[25] KINCAID, GEORGE.
Amateur footage incorporated into *President Kennedy's Last Hour*, No. 35.

Guth and Wrone No. 230.

[26] KRLD-TV, DALLAS.
Television footage of Oswald's slaying claimed by Richard Sprague but unverifiable.

See Sprague in References below.

Guth and Wrone No. 231.

[27] L'HOSTE, A. J.
Professional TV cameraman for WFAA-TV who filmed the TSBD immediately after the assassination. No record of the film appears to exist. L'Hoste was working under Malcolm Couch on the day of the assassination, see No. 16 above.

Guth and Wrone No. 233.

[28] MARTIN, JOHN H.
Amateur footage shot from the corner of Elm and Houston and incorporated into *President Kennedy's Last Hour,* No. 35, according to Guth and Wrone. However, the Department of Justice's list of films in the compilation does not mention Martin. This 10 July 1964 letter (addressed to Howard Willens) is reproduced on p253 of Weisberg's *Photographic Whitewash* (1976).

In what appears to be an FBI memo, dated sometime in 1964, it is stated that an earlier memo, dated 11 December 1963, advised that Martin took 8mm color film of the motorcade which he believed contained a view of the window of the TSBD (apparently at the time the shots were fired). The memo goes on to say that Martin's footage was obtained by *Life* magazine. This memo is reproduced in Weisberg above, p255.

Guth and Wrone No. 236

[29] MENTESANA, ERNEST CHARLES.
Color footage shot by an amateur who was standing in the freight yard near the TSBD immediately after the assassination and later by the Dal-Tex building. Partially incorporated into *President Kennedy's Last Hour,* No. 35.

An important film. One shot shows two Dallas policemen on the fire escape at the seventh floor of the TSBD gesticulating towards the roof 'as though something of great importance had been discovered.' The next shots show several police officers carefully examining a rifle that one of their number is holding. The weapon is here dubbed 'The Assassin's Rifle,' but unlike the Mannlicher-Carcano this rifle has no sight or sling and the barrel extends further beyond the stock. The shots were filmed at approximately 1.04pm, some 20 minutes before the 'Oswald' Mannlicher-Carcano was discovered.

Further confirmation of the rifle's existence was in a series of still photos taken at the time by Jim McCammon which are now lost.

The quote above is taken from Robert Sibley's article, 'The Mysterious, Vanishing Rifle of the JFK Assassination,' *The Third Decade,* September 1985. Sibley's piece is essential reading and takes in other questions about a 'second' rifle.

Mentesana ran a grocery shop on Allen Street in Dallas. He was a member of the Dallas 8mm Movie Club, the Cinema Guild of Texas, film from the members of which was edited together to produce the documentary, *President Kennedy's Last Hour,* No. 35. Mentesana died of a heart attack in 1969.

Guth and Wrone No. 237.

[30] MESTER, EARL.
Amateur footage incorporated into *President Kennedy's Last Hour,* No. 35.

Guth and Wrone No. 238.

[31] MUCHMORE, MARY.
Amateur color footage of the assassination shot from the grassy interior between
Elm and Main where Muchmore had moved after being at a position near Main
and Houston. She filmed from a position behind Charles Brehm. Her footage
shows the final fatal head shot to Kennedy and the limousine driving off under
the Triple Underpass.

Acquired by United Press International. Used wholly or partially in many
documentaries, including *The Plot to Kill Kennedy*, No. 134. UPI released the
film commercially in 1963, No. 70.

See Weisberg's *Photographic Whitewash* (1976), pps45-6.

Guth and Wrone No. 242.

[32] NIX, ORVILLE.
Color footage of the assassination shot by an amateur who was standing south of
Elm on the opposite side of the road to Abraham Zapruder. Nix's film captures
the entire assassination and shows also the limousine's brake lights coming on
prior to the head shot. Nix sold the film in 1963 to United Press International for
$5000.00, a lot less than what Zapruder received for his footage.

The film shows suspicious flashes of light on the Grassy Knoll which may be
muzzle flashes from a rifle. Some critics believe that a gunman figure can be
seen there. Nix himself thought that shots had come from this direction. In 1966
the Itek Corporation examined the film and concluded that the figure was
nothing but shadows but, as critics have pointed out, in a latter part of the film
the shadows have gone. And as Maurice Schoenfield, a UPI executive, has noted,
the Itek executives involved in the examination were ex-CIA agents.

The Warren Commission never called Nix to testify even though he had told
the FBI he was willing to appear. The Commission also chose to ignore the film.
The only interviews with Nix I know of are in the 1967 CBS documentary, No.
84, and *Rush to Judgement*, No. 85.

Nix worked for the General Service Administration as an air conditioning
repairman in the Dallas Secret Service building. He died in 1988.

The FBI established that Nix's camera ran at an average speed of 18.5 frames
per second. See J. Edgar Hoover's letter of 4 February 1964 to J. Lee Rankin
reproduced on p277 of Weisberg's *Photographic Whitewash* (1976).

On the Nix film generally see Groden and Livingstone's *High Treason*
(1989), pps192-3. An earlier but still interesting account of Nix is in Robert Sam
Anson's *"They've Killed the President!"* (1975), pps145-8 (Anson, it might be
noted, is probably the only member of the critical community ever to be a
prisoner of the North Vietnamese).

Some interesting background to the film and the story of the attempt by Nix's
daughter to regain the original (now lost apparently, and by Robert Blakey, no
less) is in Robert Hennelly and Jerry Policoff's 'JFK: How the Media
Assassinated the Real Story' that appeared in *The Village Voice*, 31 March 1992

(reprinted in Oliver Stone's *JFK - The Book of the Film* [1992], pps484-99).

A dupe of the original together with optically enlarged and enhanced versions are included in *The Day the Dream Died*, No. 147. See also *The Men Who Killed Kennedy*, No. 142. The clearest print I have seen is used in *The JFK Assassination: The Jim Garrison Tapes*, No. 174 (this documentary also includes an interview with Nix's granddaughter, Gayle Nix Jackson).

Jean-Michel Charlier, a French film-maker, obtained a good dupe from Nix's son prior to the film being handed over to the FBI. See No. 147, *The Day the Dream Died*, as noted, where an enhanced blow-up does seem to reveal a sniper on the Grassy Knoll.

UPI released the film in 1963, No. 71. Penn Jones released it in 1975, No. 98, and again in 1976, No. 109.

Guth and Wrone No. 245.

[33] OWENS, DAN.
TV cameraman listed by Richard Sprague but unverifiable.
See Sprague in References below.
Guth and Wrone No. 246.

[34] PARR, WYMAN.
Amateur footage incorporated into *President Kennedy's Last Hour*, No. 35.
Guth and Wrone No. 247.

[35] PRESIDENT KENNEDY'S LAST HOUR.
A 16mm compilation running some 12 minutes and incorporating color and b&w amateur footage of the motorcade, the assassination and its aftermath. Edited and produced by Rudolf Brenk (see No. 12 above), a member of the Dallas 8mm Movie Club.

The FBI refused the original films and ignored the compilation.

President Kennedy's Last Hour was originally produced by an amateur group in Dallas, Dallas Cinema Associates, Inc, incorporated in March 1964, that comprised members of the 'Dallas 8mm Movie Club.'

The film was later sold commercially through Wolper Productions Inc., Dallas, and used extensively in the Wolper documentary, *Four Days in November*, No. 75. All of this footage was also included in Robert Groden's film compilation, No. 104.

Incorporates footage from the following entries listed here: Nos. 7, 11, 12, 14, 21, 22, 25, 28, 29, 30, 34, 36, 38, 39, 40, 41, 42, 44 and 45.

See Weisberg's *Photographic Whitewash* (1976), pps98-107, and p241 et seq for the story of the film and its presentation to the Warren Commission.

Guth and Wrone No. 251.

[36] RANDELL, HAZEL (GOOCH).
Amateur footage incorporated into *President Kennedy's Last Hour*, No. 35.

[37] REILAND, ROLAND.
Listed as a WFAA-TV cameraman by Richard Sprague and by Weisberg in *Photographic Whitewash* (1976).
    See Sprague in References below.
    Guth and Wrone No. 254.

[38] RHODES, ALLEN.
Amateur footage incorporated into *President Kennedy's Last Hour*, No. 35.
    Guth and Wrone No. 255.

[39] SEIGLER, DR. HOWARD.
Amateur footage incorporated into *President Kennedy's Last Hour*, No. 35.
    Guth and Wrone No. 258.

[40] SHAWVER, GEORGE.
Amateur footage incorporated into *President Kennedy's Last Hour*, No. 35.
    Guth and Wrone No. 259.

[41] SPEIGLE [?].
Amateur footage incorporated into *President Kennedy's Last Hour*, No. 35.
    Guth and Wrone No. 262.

[42] THOMAS, LARRY.
Amateur footage incorporated into *President Kennedy's Last Hour*, No. 35.
    Guth and Wrone No. 264.

[43] UNDERWOOD, JAMES.
Cameraman for KRLD-TV who was riding in the press car of the motorcade. He filmed the exterior of TSBD, the Grassy Knoll and the crowds as the car moved onto Elm Street. After leaving the car he remained in front of the TSBD and filmed the activity there.
    The Warren Commission took Underwood's testimony but was uninterested in acquiring his film.
    See Weisberg's *Photographic Whitewash* (1976), pps53-8.
    Guth and Wrone No. 266.

[44] UNKNOWN - DCA-1.
Amateur footage detailed on the list supplied by Dallas Cinema Associates to the FBI of films used in the compilation of *President Kennedy's Last Hour*, No. 35.

The FBI rendered the name illegible. The document is reproduced on p254 of Weisberg's *Photographic Whitewash* (1976).
Guth and Wrone No. 268.

[45] UNKNOWN - DCA-2.
Amateur footage detailed on the list supplied by Dallas Cinema Associates to the FBI of films used in the compilation of *President Kennedy's Last Hour*, No. 35. The FBI rendered the name illegible. The document is reproduced on p254 of Weisberg's *Photographic Whitewash* (1976).
Guth and Wrone No. 269.

[46] UNKNOWN - WHITE HOUSE STAFFER.
Footage shot by a White House staffer who was three cars behind the President in the Dallas motorcade. Incorporated into *The Last Two Days*, No. 235.
Not in Guth and Wrone.

[47] WEIGMAN, DAVID.
An NBC cameraman who was in the same camera car in the motorcade as Malcolm Couch (No. 16) and who later shot b&w footage from the fore of the TSBD at the time of the assassination. The location of the footage is unknown. Ignored and/or suppressed by the FBI.
See Weisberg's *Photographic Whitewash* (1976), p123.
Not in Guth and Wrone.

[48] ZAPRUDER, ABRAHAM.
The single most important movie shot in Dealey Plaza on 22 November 1963.
Zapruder stood on the pergola north of Elm Street just to the fore of the picket fence and filmed the motorcade from its entrance onto Elm and through the assassination until the car bearing the shot President sped away under the Triple Underpass.
The color footage was shot with a Bell & Howell 8mm Director Series movie camera, Model 414 PD, Serial No. AS 13486, with a Zoomar telephoto lens. The stock was Kodachrome II. A total of 484 frames were exposed running at 18.3 frames per second. As Guth and Wrone write, No. 277, p78, the film constitutes 'a clock of the assassination, and [establishes] a time and place for much evidentiary data.'
Robert Groden has painstakingly enhanced and enlarged the film and it is his versions that are now most widely known. Another version, not the work of Groden, was shown on the *Nova* program in 1988, No. 145, and is widely regarded as the clearest version with the truest color.
Zapruder was a local clothing manufacturer who died of cancer in Dallas on 30 August 1970. *Time* said he was 65, and *Newsweek* said he was 66.
Not much is known about Zapruder. William Manchester was one of the few

writers to interview him (on 21 September 1964) and there are several references in Manchester's *The Death of a President* (1967). Zapruder was originally from Manhattan and moved to Dallas at some unspecified date before the assassination. His offices were on Dealey Plaza just across from the TSBD, on the fourth floor of the Dal-Tex Building. He was a wholesale distributor of ladies' dresses allegedly bearing the label 'Jennifer of Dallas' (I write *allegedly* as no one ever seems to have seen one. See the article by Timothy Cwiek noted below).

Zapruder was called as a witness by the Warren Commission and his testimony is printed verbatim in the 26 volumes of *Hearings*. For a discussion of his testimony and Wesley J. Liebeler's limp questioning see Weisberg's *Whitewash II* (1966), pps212-28. For a TV interview with Zapruder, by CBS, see No. 84.

Zapruder had sold his film to *Life* magazine by Monday, 25 November 1963. He claimed he only received $25,000 and gave the sum to the Firemen's and Policemen's Benevolence [*sic*] with the suggestion that it be used for Mrs Tippit. As we now know he actually received over $150,000. *Life* magazine promptly put the film under lock and key and were it not for Jim Garrison's subpoenaring of Time-Life for the film in the Clay Shaw trial there it would have probably remained for a good many more years with public access denied.

Paul Rothermel, Jr., for many years H. L. Hunt's security chief, claims that he obtained a pristine print the day after the assassination for Hunt, before Time-Life got their print (see Dick Russell's *The Man Who Knew Too Much* [1992], p584).

In 1975 Robert Groden and Dick Gregory approached Geraldo Rivera with a good clean print of the film that Groden had optically enhanced and Rivera showed it on ABC's *Goodnight America* on 6 March. Thus the first national showing of the film occurred 12 years after the assassination, on television (see No. 99).

Life sold the film back to the Zapruder family in 1975 shortly after the Rivera show for $1.00. Abraham's son, James Lorin Silverberg, a Washington tax lawyer, now does a 'brisk business' hiring it out: Oliver Stone is reputed to have paid $40,000.00 for using it in *JFK*.

See: Sylvia Meagher's *Accessories After the Fact* (1967), pps27-35, reprinted in Scott, Hoch and Stetler's *The Assassinations* (1976); Josiah Thompson, *Six Seconds in Dallas* (1967), still, after all these years, an essential work, and containing two valuable appendices by William Hoffman on the Zapruder film; *Life-Itek Kennedy Film Assassination Analysis* (1967); Weisberg, *Photographic Whitewash* (1976); Robert Groden's 'A New Look at the Zapruder Film,' *Rolling Stone,* 24 April 1975, and reprinted in Blumenthal and Yazijian's *Government by Gunplay* (1976), pps3-9.

Guth and Wrone, p78, list all of the relevant literature up to 1979. For more recent discussions see Hurt, *Reasonable Doubt* (1986), Lifton, *Best Evidence*

(1980 and 1988), and Timothy Cwiek's piece, 'Abraham Zapruder: A New Interpretation,' in the July 1987 issue of *The Third Decade* which also contains an interesting discussion of the film's chain of possession. Jim Marrs' *Crossfire* (1989) contains a good account of the film, pps64-9, and includes mention of David Lifton's view that the film may have been tampered with by the CIA's National Photo Interpretation Center, possibly on the night of the assassination. Two further works by Robert Groden co-authored with others are essential: with Peter Model, *JFK: The Case for Conspiracy* (1976), and with Harrison E. Livingstone, *High Treason* (1989), pps185-92. Livingstone's *High Treason 2* (1992) has a chapter examining the film, Chapter 17, pps357-73.

Of essential interest too is Philip H. Melanson's pioneering inquiry, 'Hidden Exposure: Cover-Up and Intrigue in the CIA's Secret Possession of the Zapruder Film,' in *The Third Decade*, November 1984.

Richard B. Stolley, Los Angeles Bureau Chief of *Life* magazine in 1963, was sent to Dallas to cover the Kennedy visit and after the assassination bought the film from Zapruder for Time-Life. His account of the transaction together with a weak defense of Time-Life's handling of the film is included in his article, 'The Zapruder Film: Shots Seen Round the World,' *Entertainment Weekly*, 17 January 1992 (reprinted in Oliver Stone's *JFK - The Book of the Film* [1992], pps410-3).

The reality of Time-Life's handling of the film is admirably detailed in Robert Hennelly and Jerry Policoff's 'JFK: How the Media Assassinated the Real Story' that appeared in *The Village Voice*, 31 March 1992 (included in Stone's *JFK, op cit,* pps484-99).

Most documentary compilations of the last ten years or so include the Zapruder film (as, indeed, did Oliver Stone's *JFK*). A recent film that contains the original together with enhanced and enlarged slowed versions (and with the Dictabelt recording synced in) is *The Day the Dream Died*, No. 147. See also below, *The Third Decade Research Conference*, No. 166, for the note on Vincent Palamara's more recent work on enhancement. The 1992 video documentary, *The JFK Assassination: The Jim Garrison Tapes*, No. 174, includes a very sharp and crisp version, probably the best I have seen.

The film was released in (bootlegged?) versions by Penn Jones in 1972 and 1976, Nos. 96 and 109.

Guth and Wrone No. 277.

3

Parkland, Love Field, Dallas Post-Assassination

In chronological order within subject areas.

[49] Parkland Hospital Exteriors.
Much newsreel footage was shot at Parkland after the arrival of JFK, chiefly of the crowds gathered there, and most of the major documentaries discussed below include shots.

[50] Parkland Doctors: Press Conference.
This is the famous press conference given at Parkland Memorial Hospital in Dallas at around 2pm after the death of President Kennedy. Present were Drs. Kemp Clark and Malcolm Perry (a photograph of the two doctors with White House staff member Wayne Hawkes and White House stenographer 'Chick' Reynolds is reproduced as Photo 14 in David Lifton's *Best Evidence* [1980]).

All the film and videotape of this important event apparently vanished. The Warren Commission itself tried unsuccessfully to locate the footage and was told by James J. Rowley of the Secret Service that not only could the film not be found but that the transcripts also were no longer in existence (see Mark Lane's *A Citizen's Dissent* [1968], p92). David Lifton subsequently found a copy of the transcript some years later.

WBAP-TV was at least one local station which shot the press conference. Dallas Secret Service Chief Sorrels included this in a TV inventory he sent to the FBI. This advised that if it were not required the station would wipe the tape and use it again. This they apparently did. See No. 61.

Two mute clips of the press conference are included in *Reasonable Doubt*, No. 159, showing Dr. Perry with Wayne Hawkes. *The Men Who Killed Kennedy*, No. 142, includes some intriguing footage of JFK's death being announced at Parkland.

The crucial importance of the press conference was, of course, Dr. Perry's description of the neck wound as an entry wound, an announcement repeated by the White House Assistant Press Secretary, Malcolm Kilduff, in No. 280.

[51] Malcolm Kilduff at Parkland.
Several documentaries contain short mute clips of the White House Assistant Press Secretary Malcolm Kilduff announcing Kennedy's death. *The JFK Assassination: The Jim Garrison Tapes* includes the film with sound, No. 174. See also No. 280.

[52] Dr. Robert Shaw at Parkland Hospital.
Dr. Shaw was Governor Connolly's surgeon. He announced the Governor's condition at a press conference.
   Sound footage is included in *Rush to Judgement*, No. 85, and mute in *The Day the Dream Died*, No. 147.

[53] Parkland Hospital to Love Field.
Newsreel shots of the body being driven from Parkland to Love Field are included in *Ruby and Oswald*, No. 119, and *The Men Who Killed Kennedy*, No. 142.

[54] Love Field.
The departure of Air Force One was well covered by the newsreel companies. Footage is included in most documentaries.

[55] Andrews AFB.
Most documentaries include b&w shots of the casket being unloaded, all of which seem to be from the same source.

[56] JFK Autopsy: Bethesda Naval Hospital.
An official film record of the autopsy was made according to some sources, by Lt. William B. Pitzer. See No. 228.

[57] Tippit Scene of Crime.
Two b&w clips taken at the site of the Tippit slaying are included in *Reasonable Doubt*, No. 159, below. From the evidence of the investigating officers present and the number of police cars it would seem this footage was shot within an hour or two of the shooting, probably by a local TV company. Essentially the same footage is shown in *The Men Who Killed Kennedy*, No. 142, and *The JFK Assassination: The Jim Garrison Tapes*, No. 174.

[58] Oswald's Arrest: Texas Theater.
The Men Who Killed Kennedy, No. 142, and *The JFK Assassination: The Jim*

Garrison Tapes, No. 174, contain b&w footage of the Texas Theater taken during or immediately after Oswald's arrest. Clips are also used in other productions.

[59] Oswald at Dallas PD.
A full catalog of Oswald footage while in police custody has yet to be made. All documentaries listed below contain some material. *The Men Who Killed Kennedy,* No. 142, is the only documentary that includes footage of Oswald being driven into the Dallas PD headquarters after his arrest.

[60] The Oswald-Ruby Slaying.
Three versions of the Oswald murder appear to have been filmed. These are:

KRLD-TV, Dallas: b&w video.
KRLD-TV, Dallas: 16mm b&w. Cameraman: George Phenix.
WBAP-TV, Fort Worth: 16mm b&w. Cameraman: J. Jamison.

This listing is based upon an inventory sent by J. Edgar Hoover to J. Lee Rankin dated 20 January 1964. In all of the documentaries that follow only two versions are ever utilized. It may be that the two KRLD-TV versions listed here are one and the same.
The longest 'take' of the slaying is included in *Assassination!,* No. 176, and includes 'live' commentary.
Jamison is noted above, No. 24.
The Hoover inventory is reproduced on pps280-1 of Weisberg's *Photographic Whitewash* (1976).

[61] WBAP-TV, Dallas.
Dallas Secret Service Chief Forrest V. Sorrels forwarded to Washington an inventory of all the footage shot and held by this Dallas TV station amongst which were interviews with the Parkland doctors. Sorrels wrote, 'WBAP-TV advised that they will hold this tape for us until the President's Commission makes a determination if they want a copy of it. If the Commission does not want a copy of it, they plan to erase it and use it over again.'
This Secret Service memo dated 18 May 1964 says the station's footage includes: 'Oswald shooting; NBC news re-enactment of Oswald's shooting; Doctors talking about Oswald at Parkland; Interview with Chief Stevenson and Chief Curry reference charges, etc. on Oswald; Tippit funeral.'
Some WBAP-TV coverage is included in No. 67, *The Kennedy Assassination: As It Happened.*
See Weisberg's *Whitewash II: The FBI-Secret Service Cover-up* (1966), p331. The memo is reproduced on p264 of Weisberg's *Photographic Whitewash* (1976).

[62] WFAA-TV, Dallas.
The inventory of footage compiled by this station (the local ABC affiliate) ran to some 26 sheets and was included in the Sorrels communication to the FBI mentioned in the previous entry. The WFAA listing was compiled by Joe Graham, a station employee. It was indexed and gave timings. Amongst the more provocative items:

> 'Secret Service quotes indicate automatic weapon used.'
> 'Bulletin - Secret Service believes that an automatic weapon was fired from the top of the knoll.'

The search of the TSBD was also covered, there were interviews with the Parkland doctors, and interviews with Oswald in police custody.

Weisberg in *Photographic Whitewash* (1976), pps265-70, reproduces memos between J. Lee Rankin and A. Goldberg which discuss the station's footage. Goldberg writes an enthusiastic memo dated 25 May 1964 urging Rankin to obtain the station's tapes and the following paragraph is worth quoting in full:

> I have reviewed the index of tapes from WFAA-TV and believe that the tapes might reveal new information and permit checking of statements made by witnesses. For instance, in Supplement, PKA-5-2, a reporter, Vic Robertson, recollects that Jack Ruby attempted to enter Captain Fritz's office while Oswald was being interrogated. There is extensive coverage of the third floor corridor of the Police Department that might show this particular scene. It is conceivable that the shots at Parkland Hospital might show Ruby, thereby corroborating Seth Kantor's statement that Ruby was there early on the afternoon of November 22. If there is coverage in these tapes or others of the Texas School Book Depository Building and vicinity immediately after the shooting, there is a slim possibility that it might show Oswald leaving the building or area.

Goldberg's enthusiasm would come to nothing as we now well know (who was it on the Commission who said, 'We're supposed to be *closing* doors, not opening them'?).

Several collectors in the critical community have coverage on video of the whole of WFAA's live output from the Friday to the Monday (in excess of some 21 hours of transmissions).

The tapes include an interview with the Dallas police captain, Will Fritz, who was in charge of the transfer of Oswald when he was shot and contain this famous and unintentionally hilarious exchange:

REPORTER: Captain, what excuse - letting him [Ruby] get that close?
FRITZ: What excuse did he use?

REPORTER: No, what excuse do you-all have, you know, that he got that close?
FRITZ: I don't have an excuse.

All of the WFAA transmissions together with outtakes are archived in the collection at Southern Methodist University, No. 264 below.

See also Nos. 8 and 27 above, and Weisberg's *Whitewash II: The FBI-Secret Service Cover-up* (1966), p331 et seq.

[63] Jack Ruby.
WFAA-TV (Dallas) and NBC newsreel footage shows Jack Ruby in the audience amongst reporters at the Henry Wade press conference held in the Dallas PD on 23 November 1963. This was the occasion when Wade claimed Oswald was a member of the 'Free Cuba movement or whatever' and Ruby corrected him by stating that it was the Fair Play for Cuba Committee. The Free Cuba Movement was an anti-Castro movement funded by the CIA.

If we had no other evidence than this, that within 24 hours of the assassination Ruby knew who Oswald was and, moreover, knew that he was a member of the FPCC, alarm bells should have rung in the head of anyone investigating the assassination.

Aside from the Oswald slaying there is little material of Ruby included in the programs discussed below. *The Men Who Killed Kennedy*, No. 142, contains one of the most comprehensive selections of Ruby footage. No. 147. *The Day the Dream Died*, also has some rare later footage.

[64] Alexander, Steven L.
See No. 227 below.

4

TV Broadcasts: 22 November 1963 and After

[65] FOUR DAYS IN NOVEMBER: THE ASSASSINATION OF JFK.
B&w/color. Running time: 100 minutes. November 1963.

This is an edited compilation of the original 56 hours of broadcast coverage of the JFK assassination put out by CBS-TV from 22-25 November 1963. Hosted by Dan Rather. Produced by Perry Wolff.

Included is Walter Cronkite's first bulletin at 12.40pm on 22 November and 'live' reports from KRLD-TV in Dallas.

Among the reporters: Roger Mudd, Charles Collingwood, Harry Reasoner, Mike Wallace, Nelson Benton, George Herman and Bob Pierpoint.

This *Four Days in November* should not be confused with David Wolper's 1964 documentary with the same title, No. 75.

Obtainable from Collector's Archives, Canada. Order No. V-191.

[66] JOHN F. KENNEDY: A MAN OF THIS CENTURY.
B&w. Running time: 115 minutes. November 1963.

A documentary tribute to JFK broadcast by CBS-TV at 8pm on the night of the assassination. The tributes and testimonials are punctuated by 'live' coverage from Dallas (including Dan Rather for KRLD-TV).

Presented by Walter Cronkite and with reports by Eric Sevaried, George Herman, Daniel Schorr, Charles Collingwood and Harry Reasoner.

Obtainable from Collector's Archives, Canada. Order No. V-089.

[67] THE KENNEDY ASSASSINATION: AS IT HAPPENED.
B&w/color. Running time: 360 minutes. November 1963.

This is NBC-TV's original coverage of the assassination as broadcast on 22 November 1963 beginning at 1.56 (EST). The coverage starts with the initial NBC-TV report of the shooting at 12.55pm and includes the following 4 and a half hours of continuous coverage.

Included are eye-witness interviews, reports on the capture of Oswald, reports from Parkland Hospital, Love Field and Andrews AFB.

The NBC reporters include David Brinkley, Chet Huntley, Bill Ryan, Elie Abel, Robert MacNeil, Tom Pettit, Peter Hackes, Nancy Dickerson and Robert Abernethy. Dallas reporters from WBAP-TV include Charles Murphy, James Darnell and Tom Whealen.

Edwin Newman provides the contemporary commentary.

First shown on the Arts and Entertainment cable network.

Obtainable from Collector's Archives, Canada. Order No. V-190.

5

Documentary Films, TV Programs, Videos

Listed in chronological order.

[68] PATHE NEWSREEL: President Assassinated.

UK. November/December 1963.
B&w. 35mm. Running time: 4.5 minutes.

This is a 'story' that was released in late November/early December 1963 in British theaters by the now defunct Pathe weekly cinema newsreel. Narrated by Bob Danvers-Walker.

'President Assassinated' is a feature that includes general introductory footage of President Kennedy, President Kennedy and Mrs. Kennedy arriving in Dallas and being welcomed by Governor and Mrs. Connolly, the motorcade, good immediate post-assassination shots of Dealey Plaza including armed policemen, armed police entering the TSBD, various shots at Parkland Hospital, footage of the Presidential limousine with the bouquet of flowers Jackie was holding in Dealey Plaza, Lee Harvey Oswald in the corridors of the Dallas PD, Air Force One at Andrews AFB with the cask being loaded into the ambulance, speech by LBJ at Andrews AFB, funeral at Arlington.

No movie footage or still photographs are shown of the assassination itself, instead a still of the TSBD separates general motorcade shots from scenes of the aftermath. Over the TSBD shot the narrator states that this was from where the shots were fired. This coupled with the unwavering assumption of Oswald's guilt (Russian defector, Russian wife, etc) underscores how rapidly the FBI/Warren Commission line was leached to and accepted by the media, internationally as well as domestically.

The golden years of Pathe newsreels were but a memory in the early 1960s. The falling off of cinema attendances and the rise of television reduced Pathe to a shoestring operation producing little more than UK domestic feature and human interest 'fillers' rather than news. The newsreel certainly had no cameramen in Dealey Plaza on 22 November. The footage here would not have been Pathe copyright, rather it would have been licensed from an agency (or agencies) in the United States.

The newsreel was included in a British 1990 Pathe compilation, *1963: A Year to Remember,* that also included other material of JFK interest, No. 164 below.

[69] FAMILY FILM OF DEALEY PLAZA BACKGROUND JUST BEFORE SHOTS FIRED.

USA. 1963.
The 8mm Robert Hughes film. See No. 23.
    Released Dallas, 1963.
    Guth and Wrone No. 1064.

[70] [Film made by] MRS. MARY MUCHMORE.

USA. 1963.
The 8mm Mary Muchmore film. See No. 31.
    Released by United Press International, 1963.
    Guth and Wrone No. 1072.

[71] [Film made by] MR. ORVILLE O. NIX, DALLAS.

USA. 1963.
The 8mm Nix film. See No. 32.
    Released by United Press International, 1963.
    See No. 32 above.
    Guth and Wrone No. 1073.

[72] THE LAW AND LEE OSWALD.

CBS-TV, New York. 29 December 1963.
Discussion between Newton E. Minow of the Federal Communications Commission and Professor Paul Freund of the Harvard Law School.
    Guth and Wrone No. 2685.

[73] CBS NEWS EXTRA: November 22 and the Warren Report.

CBS-TV, New York. 27 September 1964.
Narrated by Walter Cronkite.

'On Sunday evening, September 27, 1964, the very day the Warren *Report* was issued CBS presented its first Warren *Report* documentary. That program was comprised of carefully edited interviews designed to provide support for the Commission's conclusions.' Thus Mark Lane in *A Citizen's Dissent* (1968), p88.

Walter Cronkite would be associated with an even grander support job for the Warren *Report,* No. 84 below.

Guth and Wrone No. 2686.

[74] JOHN F. KENNEDY: YEARS OF LIGHTNING, DAYS OF DRUMS.

USA. Released 17 October 1964. Director: Bruce Herschensohn.
Color. 16/35mm. Running time: 60/90 minutes.

A glossed life, times and death of JFK produced by a government department, the US Information Agency, and narrated by Gregory Peck. Dubbed into some 30 languages and shown in 117 countries according to Guth and Wrone.

Guth and Wrone No. 1120.

[75] FOUR DAYS IN NOVEMBER.

USA. October 1964. Director: Mel Stuart.
B&w. 16/35mm and video. Running time: 123 minutes.
Executive Producer: David L. Wolper. Narration writer: Theodore Strauss. Narrator: Richard Basehart. Music: Elmer Bernstein. Editor: William T. Cartwright. Associate Editors: David Newhouse, Nicholas Clapp. Special Photography: Vilis Lapenieks. Sound Effects: Morton Tubor. Sound engineer: Jerry Young. Production Manager: Harry Bernard. Film Coordinator: Bert Gold. Research: UPI Dallas - Bill Hampton, Jack Klinger, UPI New York - Vince O'Reilly, Mark Koven. Film and research sources: President's Commission on the Assassination of President Kennedy, Military District of Washington US Army, Library of Congress, Dallas Police Department, Dallas Cinema Associates, Parkland Memorial Hospital, British Broadcasting Company [clips from *That Was The Week That Was*], Dallas Morning News, Dallas Times Herald, WFAA-TV Dallas, KRLD-TV Dallas, KLIF Dallas, KHOU-TV Houston, WWL-TV New Orleans, KHVH-TV Honolulu, Eddie Rocco. Wolper Productions in co-operation with United Press International. Released by United Artists.

An early and important documentary compilation utilizing much contemporary Dallas and other footage and following events through to JFK's burial in Arlington Cemetery.

Four Days in November toes the Warren Commission line and unquestionably assumes that Oswald was a disaffected nut who acted alone, but after discounting this bias there is much newsreel material here of value and much of it cannot been seen elsewhere. Here under different headings is the coverage principally of interest to the critical community.

JFK: includes footage at the White House and with aides, in Florida a few days prior to the Texas trip, Air Force One from Andrews AFB to Fort Worth, scenes in Fort Worth and at hotel, Houston banquet for Albert Thomas with speeches, at Fort Worth on the morning of 22 November, Air Force One from Fort Worth to Dallas, arrival at Love Field, comprehensive coverage of the motorcade and crowd scenes (including film from the Dallas Cinema Associates compilation, No. 35), the Nix film (used after a detail from the Moorman photograph to show the assassination), good coverage of Parkland Hospital scenes, Malcolm Kilduff press announcement at Parkland (mute), the body being taken to Love Field and Air Force One taking off, arrival at Andrews AFB with the casket being unloaded (several shots), Bethesda exteriors.

OSWALD: Library footage of Oswald distributing handbills in New Orleans (Nos. 4 and 5), interior and exterior shots of Oswald's rooming house at North Beckley, interiors and exteriors of the Ruth Paine residence, route of Oswald to the Paine house on 21 November, Buell Wesley Frazier and the drive to the TS-BD on the morning of 22 November, railroad yards behind the TSBD, inside the TSBD, exteriors of the TSBD after the assassination, police searches inside the TSBD, Oswald's route on the No. 30 bus, cab ride with William Whaley, boarding house, Tippit scene of crime footage and stills, general shots of West Jefferson Blvd., Johnny Brewer in the shoe shop, Texas Theater, newsreel of actual arrest, various shots of Oswald in police custody including encounters with the press, Marina and Marguerite Oswald at Dallas PD, Henry Wade press conferences, Jesse Curry newsreel interview, Oswald slaying in the police basement, ambulance to Parkland, Oswald dead on gurney, burial at cemetery with Marina, Marguerite and his elder brother present.

JACK RUBY: Carousel Club exterior, stripper, exterior and interiors of Ruby's apartment, Dan Saffron in newsroom of the *Dallas Times-Herald* who was called several times by Ruby, footage of Ruby at the Henry Wade press conference, Western Union office, slaying of Oswald, Ruby in police custody.

DALLAS: Preparations at the Trade Mart for the JFK lunch, security planning for the motorcade by Dallas police including headquarters interior shots, driving the route and the Triple Underpass. General Edwin Walker seated at a George Wallace luncheon speech, Earle Cabell, Mayor of Dallas, at a town meeting, Chief Jesse Curry on local TV on 20 November stressing the safety of the presidential visit, interview with Richard Nixon then in Dallas at a bottlers' convention on the political significance of JFK's visit, the actual recording of a local TV daytime chat-show being interrupted with the announcement of JFK's death, scenes at the Trade Mart after the death has been announced.

INTERVIEWS: (voice-overs): Linnie Mae Randle (Mrs William Randle, Buell Wesley Frazier's sister); Buell Wesley Frazier, lived near the Paines, co-worker at the TSBD; William Whaley, cab driver; Johnny Brewer, from the shoe store near the Texas Theater; Aubrey Rike, ambulance driver; Earlene Roberts, Oswald's landlady (the only filmed interview she ever gave. She died of an alleged heart failure on 9 January 1966); Gerald L. 'Jerry' Hill, Dallas PD; Judge Sarah T. Hughes, swearing in of LBJ; newsreels of Police Chief Jesse Curry and Henry Wade, Dallas DA.

Released on video in the USA by MGM/UA Home Video, 1988.
See *New York Times*, 18 September 1964, p27.
Guth and Wrone No. 1119.

[76] JFK 1917-1963.

USA. 1964. Producer: Art Lieberman.
B&w. 25/16mm. Running time: 60 minutes.

A documentary on the life and times of JFK that includes newsreel footage of the assassination and the aftermath. Narrated by Cliff Robertson.

[77] JOHN FITZGERALD KENNEDY.

USA. 1964.
B&w. 16mm. Running time: 10 minutes.
Capitol Film Laboratories. Released by Star Film Co. 1964.
Guth and Wrone No. 1121.

[78] KENNEDY IN TEXAS.

USA. 1964.
B&w. 16mm (?). Running time: 30 minutes.

A documentary compilation containing television and newsreel footage of JFK's Texas trip, including the assassination and the aftermath. Footage is also included of the President in San Antonio, Houston and Fort Worth prior to his arrival in Dallas. News reports and eye-witness interviews are used, including newsreel of Ruby's slaying of Oswald.

[79] THE PRESIDENT'S LAST HOURS.

WFAA-TV, Dallas. 1964.
B&w. Video. Running time: 30 minutes.
  Guth and Wrone No. 1123.

[80] LEE OSWALD, ASSASSIN.
BBC TV, London. 15 March 1966. Directed by Rudolph Cartier.
B&w. Video. Running time: 100 minutes.

Adapted from the stage-play by the Munich playwright Felix Lutzkendorf.
  Guth and Wrone No. 2653.

[81] THE DEATH OF KENNEDY.

BBC TV, London. 29 January 1967. Producers: Paul Fox and Peter
Pagnamenta.
B&w. Running time: approx. 300 minutes.
Compère: Cliff Michelmore. Moderator: Kenneth Harris.

A five hour examination of the assassination that included the première of
Mark Lane and Emile de Antonio's film *Rush to Judgement* (see below, No.
85).
    Emile de Antonio had arranged the showing of *Rush to Judgement* with the
BBC and Mark Lane flew over to London to take part in the debate. But it
wasn't so much a debate as a loaded apologia for the Warren Commission. The
film was shown in four segments after each of which two Commission lawyers,
Arlen Specter and David Belin, attacked its evidence under the aegis of two
'impartial' judges, the English jurist, Lord Devlin, and an American academic,
Professor Bickel, who were both, in fact, firmly pro-Warren Commission.
    The imbalance of the program was widely condemned at the time. There
was much publicity in newspapers and magazines (including a cover story in
Oz magazine) and the broadcast had the end result of generally raising the
critical conciousness in England.
    Mark Lane's account of the fiasco is in his *A Citizen's Dissent* (1968).
    A footnote: Lane writes on p75 of *A Citizen's Dissent* that 'I was not paid a
farthing for the program.' Guth and Wrone, pxxiv, quote this and say that he
actually received one of the largest fees the BBC had then paid out: $40,000.00.
Their evidence for this? A BBC contract, 'Television Hired Film Agreement
No. HF 9981' dated 23 November 1966.
    The bibliographers are a little unfair on Lane here - the contract is for a
Hired Film and Lane does state on p74 of *A Citizen's Dissent* that 'the BBC
officials signed the contract *purchasing* the film [emphasis added] for one

showing.' It is unfortunate Lane wrote that he did not make a nickel himself yet the contract is clearly for the film and, presumably, Lane had his original backers to pay and so the 40K didn't go straight into his back pocket.
   Guth and Wrone No. 2678.

[82] PANORAMA: Jim Garrison Interview.

BBC TV, London. 17 April 1967.
   Guth and Wrone No. 2679.

[83] NBC'S WHITE PAPER: The JFK Conspiracy: The Case of Jim Garrison.

NBC TV, New York. 19 June 1967.
Presenter: Frank McGee. Producer: Walter Sheridan. Consultant: Gordon Novel.

A one hour documentary attacking Garrison who was subsequently given a half-hour right-to-reply opportunity the following month by the FCC, No. 86 below.
   INTERVIEWS: Dean Andrews; Walter Sheridan; John Cancler, convicted burglar; Miguel Torres, also a burglar; Fred Leemans, New Orleans Turkish bath owner; James Phelan, journalist.
   Parts of the interviews with Dean Andrews and Walter Sheridan from this program are included in *The JFK Assassination: The Jim Garrison Tapes*, No. 174.
   Garrison's own account of this smear-laden program (masterminded by Walter Sheridan, ex-FBI) is recounted on pps165-71 of *On the Trail of the Assassins* (1988). James DiEugenio discusses the program in some detail, including Sheridan's attempted bribery of Perry Russo, in *Destiny Betrayed* (1992).
   Declassified CIA documents reveal that the Agency was well aware of the slant of the show prior to its broadcast and may have contributed to it. See Jane Rusconi's note in *JFK - The Book of the Film* (1992), p116, and Paris Flammonde's *The Kennedy Conspiracy* (1969), pps320-1.
   Guth and Wrone No. 2691.

[84] CBS NEWS INQUIRY: The Warren Commission Report.

CBS TV, New York. 25, 26, 27, 28 June 1967.
B&w. Running time: approx. 240 minutes.
Producer: Leslie Midgely. Director: Vern Diamond. Producer in Dallas: Bernard Birnbaum. Writers: Ron Bonn, Clinton McCarty, Leslie Midgely, Stephen White. Associate Producers: Jane Bartels, Ron Bonn, Walter Lister,

Clinton McCarty, Robert Richter, Sam Roberts, Joseph Wershba, Stephen White. Film Editors: David McCruden, Jack Drescher, Jerome McCarthy, Mitchell Rudick, Herbert J. Schwarz. Film Cameramen: Walter Dombrow, Herbert J. Schwartz.

Narrated/compèred by Walter Cronkite with Dan Rather.

This series of four one hour documentaries broadcast on the CBS network was the grandest and most ambitious defence of the Warren *Report* ever mounted. According to the *TV Guide* it 'took 9 months, involved scores of people, and cost just about $500,000.' CBS in a news handout said a total of 90,000 feet of film had been shot of which only 5,300 feet was used (these two reference are taken from Mark Lane, see below).

PART 1: Broadcast Sunday, 25 June 1967.

INTERVIEWS: Lawrence Schiller (introduced as a photographic expert. No mention was made that he was formerly Jack Ruby's agent); Marina Oswald; Buell Wesley Frazier; Mrs. Linnie Mae Randle (Frazier's sister); Harold Norman; James E. Jarman, Jr.; Charles Givens; Arnold Rowland; Carolyn Walther; Amos Euins; Howard Brennan; Deputy Constable Seymour Weitzman; Patrolman Gerald L. 'Gerry' Hill; Dr Joseph D. Nicol; [?] Williams; Orville Nix; S. M. 'Skinny' Holland; Dr. Luis Alvarez; Charles Wyckoff.

PART 2: Broadcast Monday, 26 June 1967.

INTERVIEWS: Harold Norman; Bonnie Ray Williams; S. M. 'Skinny' Holland; Abraham Zapruder; James Altgens; Officer Jacks; Governor John Connally; Mrs. Nellie Connally; Charles Wyckoff; Dr. Cyril H. Wecht; Dr. Malcolm Perry; Commander James Humes; Arlen Specter; Darrell C. Tomlinson; Dr. Alfred G. Olivier; Dr. William F. Enos; Jim Garrison.

PART 3: Broadcast Tuesday, 27 June 1967.

Cronkite and Rather are joined by Mike Wallace.

INTERVIEWS: Murray Jackson; Domingo Benavides; Ted Callaway; Dr. Joseph D. Nicol; Barney Weinstein; Alice and Diana ('two of Jack Ruby's girls'); George Senator (see note below); Jim Garrison; Senator Russell Long; Lee Odom; William Gurvich; Mark Lane; William Turner.

PART 4: Broadcast Wednesday, 28 June 1967.

The three compères are joined by Eric Sevareid.

INTERVIEWS: Mark Lane; Charles Brehm; Edward J. Epstein; Arlen Specter; O. P. Wright; Marguerite C. Oswald; Commander James Humes; Warren Commissioner John J. McCloy; Dr. Seymour Lipset; Henry Steele Commager.

Note: George Senator who appeared in Part 3 was Jack Ruby's roommate. If we are to believe Ron Rosenbaum in his essay 'Taking a Darker View' in *Time*, 13 January 1992, Senator is also the man Jim Garrison believes fired the fatal head shot from the Grassy Knoll.

A full transcript of the four broadcasts including the interviews is included as an appendix in the book-of-the-series, Stephen White's *Should We Now Believe the Warren Report?* (1968). White was a writer and associate producer on the series, as has been noted above, and came from the Salk Institute.

The book attempts to do what Cronkite and CBS did but in a little more detail. As the jacket flap claims, 'By pinpointing and satisfying the seven key questions repeatedly raised in objections to the Report, it should end, once and for all, any further doubts, rumors, and speculations: The Warren *Report* is solidly supported by the evidence.'

A photographic section in the middle of the book reproduces some good photographs of fifteen of those interviewed (including the only still I know of Orville Nix).

A detailed analysis and critique of the series is presented by Mark Lane in *A Citizen's Dissent* (1968), pps88-137 and ps113-132. Lane also states that he attempted to view the unused material from the series but this was denied to him by CBS. It was later learnt that the outtakes were destroyed within several weeks of the series being transmitted (see No. 230).

More incisive critiques than Lane's are Robert Sam Anson's in his *"They've Killed the President!"* (1975), pps143-5, and Josiah Thompson's in *Six Seconds in Dallas* (1967), Appendix F, pps292-5. Essential reading on the background to the series is 'JFK: How the Media Assassinated the Real Story' by Robert Hennelly and Jerry Policoff, *The Village Voice*, 31 March 1992 (reprinted in Oliver Stone's *JFK - The Book of the Film* [1992], pps484-99) who discuss the curious role of Ellen McCloy (daughter of Warren Commission member and Wall Street fixer, John J. McCloy), then an administrative assistant to Richard Salant, head of CBS News, and who was closely involved in the production of the programs. The disgraceful treatment of Orville Nix is also detailed. For further information on Nix see the interview with his granddaughter, Gayle Nix Jackson, in *The JFK Assassination: The Jim Garrison Tapes*, No. 174.

The CBS rifle tests simulating Oswald's alleged shots from the TSBD were unreliable, or rather the interpretation of them was. See the notes by Jane Rusconi on pps126-7 of Oliver Stone's *JFK - The Book of the Film* (1992).

Guth and Wrone No. 2689.

[85] RUSH TO JUDGEMENT.

USA. June 1967. Director: Emile de Antonio.
B&w. 16mm. Running time: 122 minutes.
An Impact Films release of a Judgement Films Production. Produced by Mark Lane and Emile de Antonio. Directed by de Antonio. Commentary and narration by Lane and based upon his book, *Rush to Judgement* (1966).
Assistant director: Richard Stark. Photography: Robert Primes. Editors: Daniel Drasin, Peter van Dyke. Sound: Bill Mielche.

Released in June 1967 in the USA, though the world première had been on

BBC TV in London in January 1967 (see No. 81).

The first and the most famous documentary film challenging the findings of the FBI and the Warren Commission.

Initial financing was provided in London by the three famous figures who comprised Woodfall Films - the director Tony Richardson, the playwright John Osborne, and Oscar Lewenstein, a producer. Paul McCartney of the Beatles had agreed to write the music but Lane subsequently decided a score was unneccesary.

Rush to Judgement makes good use of ABC-TV documentary footage and includes newsreel interviews from November 1963 with Jim Leavelle, Henry Wade, and Will Fritz. Also included is newsreel of Dr. Robert Shaw's press conference at Parkland Hospital on 22 November 1963.

INTERVIEWS: S. M. 'Skinny' Holland, a railroad employee who witnessed the asassination from the railroad bridge above Elm Street, interviewed at his home in Irving and on the overpass; Wilma Tice, she had seen Jack Ruby at Parkland Hospital when JFK's death was announced; Acquilla Clemons, Tippit witness; Warren Reynolds, Tippit witness, subsequently non-fatally shot in the head in a mysterious incident; Harold Williams, who linked Tippit with Ruby; Nelson Delgado, a buddy from Oswald's Marine Corps days who testifies to Oswald's poor performance on the rifle range; Richard C. Dodd, railroad employee; James Leon Simmons, railroad inspector, in the railroad yard; Orville Nix, states that several frames were missing from his film when it was returned to him by the FBI (for the Nix film, see No. 32 above); James Tague, the bystander at the underpass who was wounded in the face during the assassination; Mary Moorman; Charles Brehm, witness, and including a contemporary interview from 22 November 1963; Nancy Hamilton, ex-Ruby employee who states that Ruby ran girls and was very close to the Dallas PD; Penn Jones, Jnr.; Joseph. W. Johnson, black pianist who worked at the Carousel Club; J. C. Price, a witness who had been standing on the roof of the United States Post Office Building in Dealey Plaza during the assassination; Lee Bowers, he was behind the fence in a railroad tower when the shots were fired and saw two suspicious men in the area and what he believed was a flash of light or a puff of smoke (five months after the interview Bowers was dead); Napoleon J. Daniels, a former Dallas police officer who saw Ruby enter the basement before slaying Oswald; and, as noted above, November 1963 interviews with Henry Wade, Jim Leavelle and Captain Will Fritz.

Interviews from *Rush to Judgement* have been included in many subsequent documentaries.

A word on two of Lane's collaborators. Daniel Drasin, the editor, had made the famous cinema-verité short, *Sunday*, back in the early 1960s, while Emile de Antonio was widely known for his earlier drama-documentary, *Point of Order*, about Senator Joe McCarthy and the Army hearings. De Antonio also made a film about Vietnam, *In the Year of the Pig*, and his last film was the minimalist *Mr Hoover and I* made shortly before his death at the age of 70, circa 1989. This last film is nearly an hour and a half of de Antonio in medium shot talking into the camera about the iniquity of J. Edgar Hoover intercut, inexplicably, with de Antonio's friend John Cage baking a loaf of bread and talking about his theories. Discounting the ineffable Cage it actually makes for a compelling piece of cinema. De Antonio says that he was a class-mate of JFK's (at Harvard) and he talks about Kennedy successfully running for the Senate in the early 1950s - successfully because his father, old man Joe, paid Senator McCarthy off to keep out of Massachusetts. The film also includes some amusing documentary footage of J. Edgar Hoover making Vice-President Richard Nixon an honorary member of the FBI.

De Antonio's papers relating to *Rush to Judgement* are housed in the Archives Division of the State Historical Society of Wisconsin in Madison and include a box of biographical information, a box of general correspondence relating to the JFK controversy, and a box on the film containing the script, production notes, publicity and so on (this collection is listed by Guth and Wrone at No. 23).

The partnership between Lane and de Antonio ended acrimoniously. Lane pirated the soundtrack of *Rush to Judgement* and de Antonio started litigation. The papers relating to this are also in the de Antonio collection.

Mark Lane's account of the making of *Rush to Judgement*, its release and subsequent fallout is in his *A Citizen's Dissent* (1968) wherein also included are extracts and details of several of the film's reviews.

Released on video in the USA in 1988 by MPI Home Video under the title of *The Plot to Kill JFK: Rush to Judgement*. Some 24 minutes were removed from the original running time. Collector's Archives offer a video of the original full-length 16mm version.

Guth and Wrone No. 1125 (reviews and references listed).

[86] JIM GARRISON: NEW ORLEANS DISTRICT ATTORNEY.

NBC-TV, New York. 15 July 1967.

Garrison's half-hour right-to-reply program protesting and correcting the dis-torted NBC program noted above, No. 83. A clip from this is included in *The JFK Assassination: The Jim Garrison Tapes*, No. 174.

See pps165-171 of Garrison's *On the Trail of the Assassins* (1988).
Guth and Wrone No. 2692.

[87] JIM GARRISON INTERVIEW.

WFAA-TV, Dallas. 9 December 1967.

Garrison interviewed by Murphy Martin.
    Guth and Wrone No. 2697.

[88] NBC: THE TONIGHT SHOW: Jim Garrison.

NBC-TV, New York. 31 January 1968.
Hosted by Johnny Carson.

Jim Garrison had a full 45 minutes with Johnny Carson. The only other guest
was the folksinger, Melanie.
    No tape of the show appears to have survived but audio tapes surface from
time to time in the critical community.
    Garrison describes the show in *On the Trail of the Assassins* (1988),
pps208-15.

[89] FAREWELL AMERICA.

France. 1967/8?
Shown on the UCLA campus on 25 November 1968 and elsewhere in the USA
to selected groups.
    The film originated in France as a disinformation exercise produced by ele-
ments of French intelligence and is based upon the book of the same name:
Farewell America by 'James Hepburn' (Vaduz, Lichtenstein: Frontiers, 1968).
    For background see *The New York Times,* 1 January 1969, p12, 'Book on
Kennedy Sees a Wide Plot: Origin of French Bestseller Remains a Mystery,' by
John L. Hess, and Warren Hinckle's *If You Have a Lemon, Make Lemonade*
(1974).
    Guth and Wrone No. 2651 (where they point out that the film's doctrines are
identical with those of the feature film *Executive Action*, No. 206).

[90] OSWALD - SELF-PORTRAIT.

USA. November 1968. Produced by the Information Council of the Americas.
B&w. 16mm?
Sponsored by Schick Safety Razor Co. Narrated by Ed Butler.
    Based upon a two-record set produced by the Information Council of the
Americas released in 1964 that included Oswald's 21 August 1963 radio debate
with Carlos Bringuier and Ed Butler.
    Guth and Wrone No. 2654.

[91] A CHILD'S EYES: NOVEMBER 22, 1963.

USA, 1968. Group IV Productions.
Color. 16mm. Running time: 8 minutes.
Released by Pathe Contemporary Films.
    Guth and Wrone No. 1117.

[92] THE FATEFUL TRIP TO DALLAS: THE ASSASSINATION OF A
    PRESIDENT.

USA. 1969.
B&w. 16mm. Running time: 7 minutes.
Produced by Arthur M. Schlesinger, Jr., and Fred Israel. New York, Chelsea
House Educational Communications.
    Guth and Wrone No. 1118.

[93] THAT DAY IN DALLAS: LBJ SPEAKS.

BBC TV, London. 2 May 1970.
    Guth and Wrone No. 2680.

[94] KENNEDY ASSASSINATION NEWSREEL FOOTAGE.

Canada. 1970.
8mm.
Released by Collector's Archives.
    Guth and Wrone No. 1065.

[95] THE SERPENT.

NET-TV, USA. 1970.
Running time: 90 minutes.
National Educational Television Playhouse.
    Quoting Guth and Wrone, No. 2656: 'A "ceremony" with a segment of styl-
ized re-enactment of the Zapruder film of the JFK murder.'

[96] ZAPRUDER MOTION PICTURE OF THE ASSASSINATION OF
    PRESIDENT KENNEDY.

USA. 1972.
B&w. 8mm.
Released by Penn Jones, Jnr., Midlothian, Texas. See No. 48 above.
    Guth and Wrone No. 1078.

[97] MIDWEEK: Did Three Assassins Kill Kennedy?

BBC TV, London. 22 November 1973.
   Guth and Wrone No. 1973.

[98] NIX MOTION PICTURE OF THE ASSASSINATION OF PRESIDENT
JOHN F. KENNEDY.

USA. 1975.
Released by Penn Jones, Jnr., Midlothian, Texas. See No. 32 above.
   Guth and Wrone No. 1069.

[99] GOODNIGHT AMERICA.

ABC-TV, New York. 6 March 1975.
The Zapruder film shown nationally in the US for the first time on the show
hosted by Geraldo Rivera. Dick Gregory and Robert Groden had brought an op-
tically-enhanced version of the film to Rivera who told ABC that either they allow him to show the film or he walks.
   See further the entry on the Zapruder film, No. 48.

[100] CBS NEWS: Lyndon Johnson Interview.

CBS-TV, New York. 24 April 1975.

CBS News showed for the first time suppressed footage from a 1969 Walter
Cronkite interview with Johnson. Here Johnson says that while he could accept
that Oswald pulled the trigger he could not be sure that Earl Warren had got
the full story and that perhaps Oswald was linked to pro-Castro Cubans out for
revenge after the Bay of Pigs. Included in part in the *48 Hours* documentary,
No. 169 (see also No. 170).

[101] CBS REPORTS INQUIRY: The American Assassins: Lee Harvey
Oswald and John F. Kennedy.

CBS-TV, New York. 25, 26 November 1975. Executive Producer: Leslie
Midgely.
Color. Running time: 100 minutes (two parts).
Narrated by Dan Rather.

An examination of the various conspiracy theories that fly in the face of
Rather's beloved Warren Commission findings. Includes the Zapruder film.
   INTERVIEWS: Josiah Thompson; Dr. Cyril H. Wecht; David Belin; Richard

Snyder; Jesse Curry; Marguerite Oswald; Warren DeBrueys, FBI; Carlos Brin-
guier; Oscar Pena, New Orleans bar owner; Robert Maheu; Dr. Alfred G.
Olivier; John Connally; Gus Rose, Dallas PD (who recounts how the New
Orleans FBI agent, Warren DeBrueys, pressured him into removing Oswald's
Minox camera from the inventory prepared by the Dallas PD), etc.

Oscar Pena claimed that he saw Oswald with the FBI agent Warren
DeBrueys on 'numerous occasions.' See Dick Russell's *The Man Who Knew Too
Much* (1992), p409.

[102] ASSASSINATION: AN AMERICAN NIGHTMARE.

ABC-TV, New York. November 1975.
Color. Running time: 60 minutes.

A documentary analysis hosted by Peter Lawford (no less) concentrating on the
assassinations of JFK and Bobby Kennedy, but also including discussion of
Martin Luther King, plus the attempted assassinations of George Wallace and
Gerald Ford.

INTERVIEWS: Allard Lowenstein; Paul Schrade; Harrison Salisbury; Dick
Gregory; George Wallace; Gerald R. Ford.

[103] 60 MINUTES: JFK Assassination.

USA. TV. December 1975.
Hosted by Mike Wallace.

Secret Service Agent Clint Hill broke down and cried after telling Wallace that
had he reacted '5/10s of a second faster' in Dealey Plaza he could have saved
the President's life.

[104] THE ASSASSINATION OF PRESIDENT JOHN F. KENNEDY [THE
    JFK FILM CHRONOLOGY, THE CASE FOR CONSPIRACY].

USA. 1975. Producer/editor: Robert Groden.
B&w. 16mm. Running time: 58 minutes.

A compilation by Robert Groden containing the Nix, Zapruder and Muchmore
films and other footage shot in Dallas on 22 November, including the Dallas
Cinema Associates film (No. 35). Also included is coverage of the autopsy and
the Warren Commission.

Groden originally produced this for educational purposes only, for the Western New England College, but the film was subsequently hijacked and
bootlegged by a dealer not a million miles away from Quebec.

[105] THE ETERNAL FRAME.

USA. 1975.
B&w? Running time: 24 minutes.
Produced by T. R. Uthco and the Ant Farm.
   Guth and Wrone No. 2649.

[106] THE TWO KENNEDYS: A VIEW FROM EUROPE.

Italy. 1975. Director/editor: Gianna Bisiach.
B&w. Running time: 100/120 minutes.
According to Collector's Archives this was the first 'major presentation' to suggest that organised crime was involved in some way with the assassination.
   Guth and Wrone No. 2657

[107] LE MYSTERE KENNEDY [The Kennedy Mystery].

France/Holland. 1976. Producer/director: Jean-Michel Charlier.
Color. Running time: 240 minutes.

A detailed study of the Warren Commission's findings and the critical aftermath that includes much rare newsreel footage from 1963. Charlier's version of the Nix film is also included in No. 147.
   INTERVIEWS: Jim Garrison; Mark Lane; Leo Sauvage; Harold Weisberg; Edward Epstein; Penn Jones, Jnr.; Fletcher Prouty; William Turner; Bernard Fensterswald; Richard A. Sprague; George O'Toole.
   See entry following.

[108] SIX SECONDS TO KILL.

USA, France/Holland. 1976.
B&w. Running time: 65 minutes.

Six Seconds to Kill has a curious origin. It appears to have been adapted from the preceeding entry, *Le Mystère Kennedy,* for audiences in the US by Sherman Grinberg Films who then distributed it.
   INTERVIEWS: Jim Garrison; Mark Lane; Leo Sauvage; Harold Weisberg; Edward Epstein; Penn Jones, Jnr.; Fletcher Prouty; William Turner; Bernard Fensterwald; Richard A. Sprague; George O'Toole.

[109] ZAPRUDER AND NIX FILMS WITH GRODEN BLOW-UPS OF THE ASSASSINATION OF PRESIDENT JOHN F. KENNEDY.

USA. 1976.
B&w. 16mm.
Released by Penn Jones, Jnr., Midlothian, Texas.
   Guth and Wrone No. 1077.

[110] THE FIFTH ESTATE: The JFK Assassination - Dallas and After: An Inquiry into the Assassination of John Kennedy.

Canadian Broadcasting Company, Toronto. November 1977. Producer: Brian McKenna.
   Color. Running time: 45 minutes.

An issue of the CBC program, *The Fifth Estate,* analysing and discussing the various conspiracy theories surrounding the JFK assassination. Hosted by Peter Dale Scott, according to Collector's Archives, and by Adrienne Clarkson in Guth and Wrone (below).
   INTERVIEWS: Fletcher Prouty; William Attwood; Dr. Cyril H. Wecht; Josiah Thompson; Jack Anderson; Jesse Curry; Frank Sturgis; Gerry Patrick Hemming; William Gaudet; Ed Butler; Carlos Bringuier; Seth Kantor; Louis Kutner.
   Guth and Wrone No. 2684.

[111] ASSASSINATION USA: CONVERSATIONS.

New York access cable TV. 1977.
B&w. Running time: 360 minutes.

This is a collection put out by Collector's Archives of interviews conducted by Ted Gandolfo on the New York cable show, *Assassination U.S.A.*
   INTERVIEWS: Richard A. Sprague; Dr. Cyril H. Wecht; Michael Eddowes; Mark Lane.
   Source: Collector's Archives.

[112] THE TRIAL OF LEE HARVEY OSWALD.

ABC-TV, New York, 1977. Director: David Greene.
Color. Running time: 185 minutes.
Executive Producer: Charles Fries. Executive in Charge of Production: Malcolm Stuart. Producer: Richard Freed. Supervising Producer: Lawrence Schiller. Director of Photography: Vilis Lapenieks. Writer: Robert E.

Thompson. Art Director: Joel Schiller. Supervising Editor: Michael Economou. Editor: Allan Jacobs. Music: Fred Carlin. 'Based upon an original Broadway stage play, *The Trial of Lee Harvey Oswald,* written by Amram Ducovny and Leon Friedman.' Charles Fries Productions Inc. Worldvision Enterprises Inc. CAST: Ben Gazzara (prosecution attorney), Lorne Greene (defense attorney), Frances Lee McCain, Lawrence Pressman, Charlie Robinson, George Wyner, Mo Malone (Marina Oswald), John Pleshette (Lee Harvey Oswald), etc.

The trial of Lee Harvey Oswald as it might have taken place had he not been shot by Jack Ruby. Much of the film was shot on location, at Dealey Plaza, in the TSBD, and in Dallas elsewherc. These scenes are, by and large, superbly re-created and photographed. The trial itself is unfocussed and inconclusive and lacks credibility.

Despite the general pro-Warren tenor of the production the viewer is given enough suggestions and hints to believe that Oswald was part of a conspiracy, probably composed of intelligence and mob elements.

Richard Case Nagell has said that he was amazed how closely the actor John Pleshette resembled Oswald in this production, right down to his mannerisms: 'His facial expressions were really like Oswald. A blank stare. You didn't know if the guy was agreeing or disagreeing with you. That's typical Oswald. I don't think he ever let his emotions get the best of him. Let me tell you, he was a cool customer.' The quote comes from Dick Russell's *The Man Who Knew Too Much* (1992), p368.

Lawrence Schiller, the Supervising Producer, was for a time Jack Ruby's business agent and later co-authored, with Richard Warren Lewis (a Hollywood gossip columnist), an early and egregious defense of the Warren Commission's findings - *The Scavengers and Critics of the Warren Report* (New York: Dell Publishing, 1967). For more information about Schiller and a discussion of his book see Mark Lane's *A Citizen's Dissent* (1968), pps98-9, 198-204.

[113] TWO MEN IN DALLAS: JOHN F. KENNEDY AND ROGER CRAIG.

USA. 1977.
Color. 16mm. Running time: 60 minutes.
Narrated by Mark Lane. Alpha Productions.

A documentary examining the assassination and the events thereafter as witnessed by Deputy Sheriff Roger D. Craig of the Dallas PD.

INTERVIEWS: Roger Craig; James Hosty; Gordon Shanklin; Charles Brehm; Penn Jones, Jnr.

Craig corroborated Deputy Sheriff Boone and Seymour Weitzman's testimony that the rifle originally found in the TSBD was not a Mannlicher-Carcano but a Mauser. Earlier Craig had seen a white male running down the hill from the TSBD who then climbed into a Rambler station wagon driven by a 'dark-complected white male.' Craig said 'I tried to get across Elm Street to stop the car and talk with [the] subjects, but the traffic was so heavy I could not make it.'

Later Craig was astonished to find the individual fleeing the TSBD was in Captain Fritz's office - Lee Harvey Oswald. Fritz swore to the Warren Commission that Craig was never in his office at the time - the Dallas PD's denigration of Craig had begun. It was several years later before Craig was vindicated when Police Chief Curry published his memoires of the assassination. There amongst the photographs was a picture of Oswald being interrogated in Fritz's office - with Roger Craig present.

In 1967 Craig was dismissed from the Dallas PD for allegedly talking to Jim Garrison. He was later shot at in a parking lot. Further attempts were made on his life, including a car bombing, and in May 1975 he was found dead from a rifle wound, allegedly suicide.

See Edgar F. Tatro's 'Roger Craig and "1984"' in the May 1983 *Continuing Inquiry* newsletter. Craig's own typescript, *When They Kill a President,* is obtainable from the JFK Assassination Information Center in Dallas. The photograph of Craig in Fritz's office is reproduced in the illustrative section between pps138-9 of Henry Hurt's *Reasonable Doubt* (1986).

Guth and Wrone No. 1131.

[114] PANORAMA: Who Really Killed Kennedy?

BBC TV, London. 6 March 1978.
  Guth and Wrone No. 2682.

[115] THE TRIAL OF LEE HARVEY OSWALD.

BBC TV, London. 16 April 1978.
Original play first shown on ABC-TV, see No. 112.

[116] PEOPLE: Marguerite Oswald Interview.

WFAA-TV, Dallas. November 1978.

A lengthy conversation with Marguerite Oswald that includes discussion of the assassination and the murder of her son. Interviewer: Michael Brown.

[117] THE HOUSE SELECT COMMITTEE ON ASSASSINATIONS.

PBS-TV, Washington. 1978.

The public hearings of the House Select Committee were broadcast by PBS. These were largely devoted to the examination of witnesses and critics, usually with a commentator or expert narrating the proceedings. The total broadcast material extends to some 84 hours.

A complete set of the broadcast material is archived at the PBS library in Alexandra, Virginia (see No. 262).

Robert Blakey recently stated, with some personal pride, that the Select Committee held 18 days of public hearings. Only 18 days out of the 365 days the Committee was in session!

[118] THE KILLING OF PRESIDENT KENNEDY.

USA. 1978.
Color. Running time: 80 minutes.
Produced by Witness Productions. Released (?) by Syndicast Services, New York and Washington.
A British documentary originally entitled *The Kennedy Cover-Up: What We Know Now That We Didn't Know Then,* made by Anthony Summers and David Osterlund.
INTERVIEWS: House Select Committee members; Warren Commission staffers; Sylvia Odio.
Guth and Wrone No. 1122 (who include it under the original title).

[119] RUBY AND OSWALD [aka FOUR DAYS IN DALLAS].

USA. 1978. Director: Mel Stuart.
Originally made for and shown on US TV in 1978 (confusingly, the UK video release by Odyssey has a copyright date of 1981).
A Reeves Entertainment Group Presentation. Executive Producer: Alan Landsburg. Producer: Paul Freeman. In Charge of Production: Howard Lipstone. Writers: John McGreevey, Michael McGreevey. Photography: Matthew F. Leonetti. Art Director: Ray Beal. Editors: Corky Ehlers, George Hively. Sound Mixer: Eddie Knowles.
CAST: Frederic Forrest (Lee Harvey Oswald), Michael Lerner (Jack Ruby), Doris Roberts (Eva Ruby), Lou Frizzell (Captain Fritz), Bruce French (Robert Oswald), Sandy McPeak (Henry Wade), Lanna Saunders (Marina Oswald), Sandy Ward (Chief Curry), Richard Sanders (Agent Kelley), David Leroy Dorr (Wesley Frazier), Delbert Henry Knight, Sr. (Junior Jarman), Adrianna Shaw (Helen Markham), Lesley Woods (Ruth Paine), etc.

Color: Consolidated. Original TV running time: 156 minutes. Odyssey Video release running time: 103 minutes (though the wrapper says '90 minutes approx.').

This 'docudrama' is largely based on Warren Commission testimonies, the 'approved' testimonies, that is, included in the *Report*. It cuts between Ruby and Oswald as they go their separate ways from the morning of Thursday 21 November through to the Sunday when it ends with Ruby alone in a police cell after the slaying of the alleged assassin.

All of the main events are reconstructed including Oswald's 'curtain rods' lift into work with Frazier, the encounter with Officer Baker and Roy Truly at the soft-drinks machine on the TSBD's second floor, the bus and taxi rides back to Oak Cliff, the shooting of Tippit (as per the *Report*), the subsequent arrest in the cinema, the hours in police custody according to the Dallas PD's version and then the basement shooting by Ruby (who is shown coming down the ramp!).

Despite good performances by Forrest and Lerner the film never quite struggles free of the eye-witness testimony that it is based upon. Oswald is a cipher throughout, you never know what he's thinking, where he's coming from, whereas the presentation of Ruby subscribes totally to the Warren Commission's view and not even an actor as good as Lerner can make it convincing. We are given a Ruby who is in love with his President and the liberal ideals he stands for, a nightclub owner who is outraged by the slightest criticism of Kennedy and, essentially, a home-loving family sort of guy who is paranoid about antisemitism. The only time Lerner manages to sneak in something approaching the real Ruby is at the press conference where he corrects Wade's statement about Oswald's involvment with a pro-Cuba group. After Lerner says 'Fair Play for Cuba Committee' there is a smirky smile on his face that says more about the real Ruby than the rest of the film. Here's the face of the conpiratorial hood who knows more than he ever wanted to know, the hoodlum with the inside track.

If the dramatic narrative of Ruby and Oswald lacks interest there are, however, two compelling reasons for viewing the film.

Ruby and Oswald was shot in Dallas at the actual scenes and locations of the story and unlike nearly every other film described here conveys a very real sense of place. The high angle panning shot of Dealey Plaza at the beginning of the film, the drives along the freeways, the Oak Cliff area, inside the TSBD and the area behind it (overgrown and abandoned railway tracks with the signal box some distance off) are some of the shots that convey the authentic topography and feel of the place.

Intercut with the Ruby/Oswald narrative is a considerable body of newsreel footage of Kennedy taken at the time, more so than in most films discussed herein. Much of it is vignetted in a TV mask. It begins with JFK leaving

Andrews AFB in Air Force One for the Texas trip, a speech in Houston, very extensive coverage of the arrival at Love Field and the passage of the motorcade, Parkland Hospital (again, more shots than any other documentary listed here), the drive from Parkland to Love Field, and the return at Andrews AFB. Also included is the newsreel of Oswald distributing leaflets on 16 August 1963 outside of the Trade Mart in New Orleans, No. 4.

Released in the UK in 1989 by Odyssey/Virgin Video with a running time of 103 minutes.

[120] BEST EVIDENCE: THE RESEARCH VIDEO.

USA. 1980.
For David S. Lifton's documentary see No. 165.

[121] BLOOD FEUD.

USA, TV. 1980. Director: Michael Newell.
Color. Running time: 199 minutes.
CAST: Robert Blake, Cotter Smith, Forrest Tucker, Ernest Borgnine, Brian Dennehy, Danny Aiello, etc.

A very well made documentary-drama charting the 12-year battle between Robert and Jack Kennedy and the corrupt unions led by Jimmy Hoffa. Essential viewing on the background to the assassination.

[122] IN SEARCH OF: Lee Harvey Oswald.

USA, TV. 1980. Produced by Alan Landsburg Productions.
Color. Running time: 30 minutes.

An examination of Lee Harvey Oswald, his background and possible conspirators in the assassination.
INTERVIEWS: Robert Groden; Edward Epstein; Michael Eddowes; Dr. Barger.

[123] SPEAK-UP AMERICA: JFK Assassination Inquiry.

NBC-TV, New York. 1980.
Color. Running time: 25 minutes.

INTERVIEWS: Jim Leavelle; L. C. Graves; Dr. Robert McClelland; Dr. Roy C. Jones; Jim Garrison; Louis Stokes; Marguerite Oswald; Penn Jones, Jnr.; Phil Willis; Mark Lane.

[124] THE FIFTH ESTATE: The Missing Casket.

Canadian Broadcasting Company, Toronto. April 1981. Producer: Brian
McKenna
Color. Running time: 30 minutes.

This documentary examining the 'two casket' theory is mentioned by David
Lifton in the 1988 edition of *Best Evidence,* p701-2. Lifton interviewed Donald
Rebentisch of Coopersville, Michigan, a petty officer at Bethesda in November
1963 who confirmed the two ambulance story. The film's producer also discovered unedited footage of Air Force One at Andrews AFB which reveals the
presence of a helicopter on the far side that takes off shortly after the
presidential plane lands (carrying, according to Lifton's thesis, JFK's body).
Some rare footage is also included of Bethesda Naval Hospital.
    INTERVIEWS: David S. Lifton; Don Rebentisch.

[125] JACQUELINE BOUVIER KENNEDY.

ABC-TV, New York. 14 October 1981. Director/writer: Stephen Gethers.
Color. Running time: 180 minutes.
Producer: Louis Rudolph. An ABC Circle Film.
CAST: Jaclyn Smith (Jacqueline Bouvier Kennedy), James Franciscus (John F.
Kennedy), Rod Taylor (John 'Blackjack' Bouvier), Stephen Elliott (Joseph
Kennedy), Will Hunt (Theodore White), etc.
First shown in the UK on 2 May 1983 by ITV/Yorkshire Television.
The story of Jackie from the age of five until immediately after the
assassination in 1963. A quote from the publicity release put out by Yorkshire
Television in the UK before the screening gives a good idea from whence this
production comes: 'When she eventually became the First Lady, Jackie dazzled
the country with her style and taste. She became the nation's leading
trendsetter, and a feature of the film is the collection of 78 different costumes
Jaclyn [Smith] wears. They were valued at more than 250,000 dollars.'
    The dialogue like everything else in this production is risible. An example:
'It's a *fait accompli*,' declares a young Jackie over the dinner table. 'Oh, you
speak French!' exclaims Senator Kennedy. An exchange that prompted the
critic in *Variety* (21 October 1981) to note that if she had sneezed he would
have thought she spoke German.
    The assassination is not shown but is recalled by Jackie in conversation with
Theodore White (the first screen portrayal of White, I believe).

[126] OSWALD EXHUMATION/AUTOPSY VIDEOS.

Dallas, Texas. 1981.
Color. Running time: approx. 240 minutes.

Some four hours of video tape were made of the exhumation and autopsy performed on Lee Harvey Oswald in 1981. The exhumation arose from the claims
by the English lawyer, Michael Eddowes, that the Oswald who returned from
Russia was an impostor.

Eddowes entered into an agreement with Marina Oswald Porter for the production of the videos and as late as 1986 there were still legal squabbles with
the two cameramen who shot the footage (see *The Third Decade,* January
1987).

The videos were produced for Eddowes and Porter by Hampton Hall, the son
of a Texas state politician.

Eddowes is the author of *The Oswald File* (1977). He has been virtually sole
champion of the theory that the Russians were responsible for the assassination.
For some interesting background on Eddowes and his involvement on the
periphery of the British sex scandal, the Profumo Affair, see Tony Summers
and Stephen Dorril's *Honeytrap: The Secret World of Stephen Ward* (London:
1988).

Numerous shots of the exhumation together with a shot of Dr. Linda
Norton, the pathologist, discussing her findings at a press conference are
included in *The Men Who Killed Kennedy,* No. 167, Part 2. It isn't known
whether this material came from the cameramen employed by Eddowes and
Porter. The exhumation is also discussed in No. 168.

The best and most balanced account of the exhumation is in Jim Marrs'
Crossfire (1989), pps546-53. Marrs includes the doubts of Paul Groody and
Alan Baumgartner arising from the disinterment.

[127] NBC NEWS: John F. Kennedy Remembered.

NBC-TV, New York. 1982. Director: Tom Priestley.
B&w. Running time: 58 minutes.
Writer: Lou Hazam. Editor: Constantine S. Gochis. Photography: LeRoy
Anderson. Narration: Frank McGee. Correspondent segments: David Brinkley,
Sandy Vanocur, Ray Scherer, Edwin Newman, Chet Huntley. Associate
producer: Daniel Karasik. Produced by Lou Hazam.

A scissors-and-paste documentary tracing JFK's final journey from the Capitol
to Arlington Cemetery with intercut flashbacks of various speeches and press
conferences. Includes the whole of Kennedy's swearing-in and inaugural
address (with JFK in a silk top hat and striped pants).

The film scrupulously ignores the assassination and is noted here merely to scotch the belief that it contains the Nix and Zapruder films.

In 1990 the documentary was repackaged and reissued by Castle Communications in England as a volume in the video series *Men of Our Time* (the other subjects are Lenin, Hitler, Mussolini, and Gandhi). The title was changed to *Kennedy: JFK Remembered.*

The liner notes on the video cover echo the view that the circumstances surrounding Kennedy's death are not, in the words of Anthony Sadleir, a fit subject for speculation by responsible gentlemen: 'The manner of Kennedy's death has provided the subject matter for all too many documentaries'[!].

[128] KENNEDY.

UK, Central TV. 20, 21 and 22 November 1983. Director: Jim Goddard.
Color. Running time: 313 minutes.
Supervising Producer: Joan Barnett. Executive Producer: Margaret Matheson.
Producer: Andrew Brown. Script: Reg Gadney. Photography: Ernie Vincze.
Production Design: Ben Edwards. Music: Richard Hartley. Supervising Editor:
Ralph Sheldon. A Production of Central Independent Television PLC in
association with Alan Landsburg Productions Inc.
CAST: Martin Sheen (JFK), John Shea (Robert Kennedy), E.G. Marshall
(Joseph Kennedy), Vincent Gardenia (J. Edgar Hoover), Blair Brown
(Jacqueline Kennedy), Nesbit Blaisdell (Lyndon B. Johnson), Kevin Conroy
(Edward Kennedy), Peter Bogden (Pierre Salinger), Charles Brown (Martin
Luther King), J. R. Dusenberry (Governor Connally), Margo Tully (Nellie
Connally), Harry Madsen (Clint Hill).
Released in the UK on video in a two tape boxed set by Central Television Enterprises in association with Video Collection International Ltd, April 1992.

If Leon Uris were to have written a novelization of the Kennedy presidency this is the film that would have been based upon it; a vast, sprawling production that reduces everything and everybody to the conventions of glossy popular fiction. This is history trivialised and reworked as an episode of *Dynasty* or some similar glitzy soap.

Martin Sheen believes statesman-like gravitas is conveyed by speaking slowly and pronouncing every word individually and precisely (he frequently sounds more like Winston Churchill than JFK) while Blair Brown as Jackie remains in terminal cutesie mode throughout and does little more than add to the set dressing, a pity because she is not untalented, but then in schlock like this, who needs talent? Nesbitt Blaisdell as LBJ gives what may be the best screen portrayal to date of the hoary old Texan. He conveys that strange mixture of crassness and sensitivity that the VP made all his own. A good word too for Harry Madsen as Clint Hill who in the Dealey Plaza sequence has few words but more presence than most of the rest of the cast put together.

The build-up to the assassination is handled very effectively: Air Force One arrives at Love Field and the motorcade moves off to downtown Dallas. There's an unease in the air. But the finale is anti-climactic. Sheen grasps his throat and falls forward, shots ring out, and that's that. The assassination is over. We never see Sheen/JFK again as his head is covered by a jacket and, of course, none of the controversy surrounding the shooting is addressed. Then the Presidential limousine arrives at Parkland Hospital, but this Parkland looks more like a hospital up an alley off East 100th Street. It is done in a tight shot and one wonders if the production after running out of ideas now ran out of money.

[129] GOOD MORNING, AMERICA: November 22, 1963.

ABC-TV, New York. 22 November 1983.

An anniversary tribute to JFK featuring interviews with many of his aides and colleagues. Notable for including the first public showing of the hitherto un-known Chris Darrouzet film of the motorcade in Dallas, No. 19.

[130] JFK: THE DAY THE DREAM DIED.

WFAA-TV, Dallas. 22 November 1983.
Color. Running time: 30 minutes.

A look-back upon the assassination by a local Dallas TV company that includes twentieth anniversary reports by NBC and ABC television companies.
    INTERVIEWS: David S. Lifton; Mary Ferrell; Penn Jones, Jnr.

[131] THE KENNEDY TAPES.

WFAA-TV, Dallas. 22 November 1983.
A local documentary.

[132] THE FIFTH ESTATE: Who Killed JFK?

Canadian Broadcasting Corporation, Toronto. 1983.
Color. Running time: 60 minutes.

An investigation into the conspiracy theories surrounding the case.
    INTERVIEWS: Dr. Cyril H. Wecht; Peter Dale Scott; Fletcher Prouty; Robert Groden; David S. Lifton; Bernard Fensterwald; Richard Billings.

[133] NIGHTLINE: JFK Assassination: Conspiracy Theories.

ABC-TV, New York. 1983.
Color. Running time: 60 minutes.

Discussion of theories surrounding the assassination on the ABC-TV program
hosted by Ted Koppel.
    INTERVIEWS: David Belin; Mark Lane; Louis Stokes; Ron Rosenbaum.

[134] THE PLOT TO KILL PRESIDENT KENNEDY: FROM THE DE-
    CLASSIFIED FILES.

USA. 1983. Producer/writer: John Sharnik.
Color. Video. Running time: 58 minutes.
Producer, writer: John Sharnik. Executive producer: M. G. Hollo in association
with Fox/Larber Associates Inc. Associate Producer, Editor: Howard Mann.
Narrator: Larry McCann. Camera: Raymond Grosjean. Sound: George Meune.
Acknowledgements to: Witness Productions Inc., M. G. Hollo, David
Osterlund, Anthony Summers. Copyright 1983 M. G. Hollo Co.
    Released by VidAmerica in the USA, 1983 (re-released in 1989).

A curious and scrappily produced documentary pointing the finger at the
Mafia. The best part of the production is the contemporary newsreel footage,
this includes the motorcade, color shots at Parkland, Jesse Curry and Henry
Wade press conferences, Oswald in custody and the slaying, Ruby's trial and
the final interview shortly before his death (though not shown complete). The
Nix and Muchmore films are also used.
    In support of the Mafia thesis newsreel is included of Santos Trafficante,
Jimmy Hoffa and JFK, and Sam Giancana.
    INTERVIEWS: Richard Schweiker; Gerry Patrick Hemming, who says he was
offered money several times to assassinate JFK, mainly by right-wingers;
Carlos Bringuier; Antonio Veciana; Sylvia Odio, in silhouette; William
Gaudet, witness to Oswald being with Guy Bannister; 'Dr. Peters' (pseudonym),
present at a Miami meeting with Johnny Roselli and Sam Giancana, says
Robert Maheu put out the Castro contract on behalf of the CIA; Hawk Daniels,
ex-FBI officer on wire-tapping the Teamsters; Robert McKeown, a Ruby
contact who had run guns to Cuba (see David E. Scheim's *Contract on America*
[1988], pps199, 200, 202, and 431, note 46 for Chapter 16).

[135] CALL TO GLORY: JFK.

ABC-TV, New York. 1985. Director: Peter Levin.
Color. Running time: 90 minutes.

CAST: Keenan Wynn, J.D. Cannon, Craig T. Nelson, Cindy Pickett, etc.

A drama-doumentary concerning a U-2 pilot and the escalation of the war in Vietnam intercut with the assassination of JFK and utilizing Dallas newsreel footage. The characters are from the cancelled TV series of the same name.

[136] THE TWILIGHT ZONE: Profile in Silver.

CBS-TV, New York. March 1986.
Color. Running time: 27 minutes.
Producer: Harvey Frand. Director of Photography: Chuck Arnold. Director: John Hancock. Writer: J. Neil Schulman. Executive Story Consultant: Alan Brennert. Production Designer: Ward Preston. Editor: Noel Rogers. Music: Basil Poledouris.
CAST: Andrew Robinson, Lane Smith, Louis Giambalvo, Barbara Baxley, Jerry Hardin, Mark Taylor, Charles Lanyer, David Sage, Ken Hill, etc.

An episode in the popular television series telling the story of an historian (and direct descendent of JFK), Dr. Joseph Fitzgerald, who travels back in time from the year 2172 to study the JFK presidency. Fitzgerald goes to Dealey Plaza and averts the assassination only to find that another 'time line' develops in which Khrushchev is assassinated on the same day and the Russians invade Berlin. The only way atomic war can be averted is by history being 'reinstated' and the President being assassinated in Dallas on 22 November 1963. Fitzgerald exchanges places with JFK and *he* is shot on Elm Street instead. JFK travels forward in time and becomes a Harvard historian in the 21st century.

[137] DOUBLE IMAGE [YURI NOSENKO, KGB].

BBC TV, London. 6 April 1986. Director: Mick Jackson.
Color. Running time: 90 minutes.
First shown on BBC2 TV in the 'Screen Two' series as *Double Image*. US broadcast on 7 September 1986 by HBO retitled as *Yuri Nosenko, KGB*.
Production company: BBC TV in association with Primetime TV. Executive producer: David Elstein. Producer: Graham Massey. Writer: Stephen Davis. Music: Peter Howell. Photography: David Feig.
CAST: Tommy Lee Jones (Steve Dalley), Oleg Rudnik (Nosenko), Josef Sommer, Ed Lauter, Alexandra O'Karma, Stephen D. Newman, etc.

The defection of the KGB officer Yuri Nosenko to the USA in 1964 and his promise of important information on Lee Harvey Oswald and the assassination of Kennedy (not to mention the moles in the CIA) is a fascinating and complex affair expertly handled by Stephen Davis in his screenplay. This is an effective dramatization that owes much to the fine acting of Tommy Lee Jones as Steve Dalley, the CIA case officer investigating Nosenko (Jones was later to play Clay Shaw in Oliver Stone's *JFK*).

Stephen Davis also wrote the screenplay for John Mackenzie's lamentable 1992 movie, *Ruby* (No. 226).

The two basic texts on Nosenko are David Martin's book, *The Wilderness of Mirrors* (1980), and the article by Ron Rosenbaum in the October 1983 *Harper's*, 'The Shadow of the Mole'. Edward Epstein has much on the subject in *Legend: The Secret World of Lee Harvey Oswald* (1978), some of which may be reliable. See also Anthony Summers' *The Kennedy Conspiracy* (1989), pps164-73.

[138] THE TRIAL OF LEE HARVEY OSWALD.

Channel 4 TV, London. 23 November 1986. Director: Ian Hamilton.
Color. Running time: 294 minutes.
First shown in US on Showtime Cable TV on 21 and 22 November 1986.
PART 1: The Prosecution. Running time: 163 minutes.
PART 2: The Defense. Running time: 131 minutes.
Executive Producer: Richard Drewett. Producer: Mark Redhead. Senior Cameraman: Dave Taylor. Vision Controller: Terry Pyrke. Vision Mixer: Paul Wheeler. Stage Manager: Peter Tyrell. Floor Manager: Ken Hounsom. Make up: Janis Gould. Assistant Designer: David Reekie. Graphic Designer: Tony Oldfield. Videotape Editor: Graham Sisson. Sound Supervisor: Bob Bell. Lighting Director: Colin Innes-Hopkins. Designer: Bryan Bagge. Film and Stills Research: Steve Stevenson. Research: Kerry Platman, Richard Tomlinson. With Special Thanks to: Anthony Summers, Marion Johnson, The National Archives, Washington DC, Mary Ferrell, Bill Bancroft, British Caledonian Airways. Film excerpts courtesy of: KTVT-TV, Fort Worth, Mrs. Maureen Hughes.

The Judge: The Honorable Lucius D. Bunton. Prosecuting Attorney: Vincent T. Bugliosi. Defense Attorney: Gerry Spence, with Edward P. Moriarty. Clerk: Kenneth Nelson. Marshall: Don Fellows. Deputy Marshall: Steve Rome.

Introduced by Edwin Newman (with, in the US version only, Jack Anderson, Ramsey Clark and Alan Dershowitz adding commentary).

The idea of staging a trial of Lee Harvey Oswald with a real judge and real prosecuting and defense attorneys is one of those TV producer's ideas that looks good in a production meeting but then evaporates in the realization. It would have been a good program if only.... The limitations are immediately apparent: not enough witnesses and not enough time confounded by the agendas of the attorneys. One wants to convict him and the other wants him found innocent.

The truth, if it does emerge, seems to be a by-product of legal manoeuvreing (I am reminded of what a lawyer once said to me when I asked him what the best definition of evidence was. He replied in a snap, 'Whatever you can get the jury to believe.'). Nonetheless, *The Trial of Lee Harvey Oswald* offers some compelling viewing, not least of which is the hostile questioning by Gerry Spence of some old familiar faces (Spence, it will be remembered, represented Karen Silkwood's family in the Kerr-McGee case).

The US courtroom was built in London and all of those participating were flown over from the States, hence the appearance of British Caledonian Airways in the credits above.

The program opens with an introduction by Edwin Newman who goes over the evidence according to Earl Warren and asks a few pertinent questions. There is good color footage of JFK arriving at Love Field, the motorcade, color footage of Parkland, the Ruby shooting, shots of the Warren Commission, and color footage of the House of Representatives Select Committee in session. Also shown is an excerpt from the WDSU-TV New Orleans interview with Oswald, No. 6, the Hughes film, No. 23, and the enhanced Zapruder film at normal speed (but see below).

Part 1: THE PROSECUTION

Bugliosi's opening statement is a strident and emotive rehearsal of the Warren Report's key points complete with references to the 'fanatical Marxist' and the fact that he was a lone, mad nut. This is the mindset of people like David Belin: nothing of what has come to light in the last 30 years has ever percolated through to them. They are caught in a 1963/4 time warp. Spence's opening statement, on the other hand, would do any critic proud. In reference to Bugliosi's statement he asks the jury, 'We don't like Commie mad men, do we?' He speaks of a locked closet that will never be open, therein are the secrets we shall probably never know...because *they* don't want you to know.

WITNESSES FOR THE PROSECUTION: Buell Wesley Frazier, TSBD co-worker; Charles Brehm, Dealey Plaza witness; Harold Norman, TSBD employee; Eugene Boone, Dallas PD; Marion Baker, Dallas PD; Ted Callaway, Tippit witness; Johnny Brewer, shoe shop manager; Cecil Kirk, Select Committee photographic expert; Dr. Charles Petty, autopsy panel, House Select Committee; Monty Lutz, firearms panel, House Select Committee; Dr. Vincent Guinn, bullett analysis, House Select Committee; Lyndal L. Shaneyfelt, ex-FBI, Warren Commission photographic and handwriting expert; Nelson Delgado, with Oswald in the Marines; Ruth Paine.

The cross-examination of Cecil Kirk features repeated showings of an enhanced version of the Zapruder film and a lengthy discussion of its evidentiary value.

Part 2: THE DEFENSE

WITNESSES FOR THE DEFENSE: Bill Newman, Dealey Plaza witness; Tom Tilson, Dallas PD; Dr. Cyril H. Wecht, forensic pathologist (his spirited exchanges with Bugliosi are one of the highlights of the trial); Paul O'Connor, Bethesda orderly; James Hosty, FBI Dallas office; Edwin-Juan Lopez, attorney and researcher, House Select Committee; Seth Kantor, journalist who saw Ruby at Parkland.

Kantor's testimony includes several contemporary film clips: Oswald being shot in the Dallas PD basement, Oswald protesting his innocence while in custody, and other shots. Also included is footage of Ruby talking at a press conference at the time of his trial and saying how the world will never know the full story behind what he did.

The final summations by the two attorneys effectively demonstrate the polarization of opinion on the case. Bugliosi rehearsed the arguments of the Warren *Report*, everything was known, cut and dried (what's all the fuss about?), while Spence argued that most of the relevant evidence was still in the 'locked closet' and that the US government was determined that it should stay that way. The defense attorney also highlighted the strange coincidences of the case against Oswald, not least of which was a good examination of the evidence against Oswald emanating from the Paine household.

The evidence in a criminal prosecution must prove the guilt of the defendant 'beyond a reasonable doubt' and in view of this and the admirable presentation of the defense case by Spence it is quite surprising that the jury returned a unanimous verdict of guilty. Spence might not have proved his client was 'innocent' but he certainly battered Bugliosi's case enough to raise a reasonable doubt.

Before the end credits roll-up the following is superimposed over the Seal of the United States:

After returning a verdict of Guilty the jury was asked to consider whether Oswald had acted alone or with others. The majority concluded he was the sole assassin.

In a telephone poll of viewers conducted by Showtime cable only 15% voted Oswald guilty, the remaining 85% found him not guilty.

See Jerry D. Rose's 'Showtime's Show Trial' in *The Third Decade*, November 1986, ps16-24, for a full discussion of the witness testimonies.

Gerry Spence is the author of a fine critique of the American legal system, *With Justice for None: Destroying an American Myth* (New York: Times Books/Random House, 1989, and Penguin Books, 1990).

Jane Rusconi in the gloss to Oliver Stone's *JFK - The Book of the Film* (1992), p158, states that Dr. Pierre Finck who was present at the Bethesda autopsy appeared in the program. If he did his appearance was edited out of the version shown in England.

[139] ROBERT EASTERLING VIDEO.

USA. Video. Circa 1986.

On p5 of the January 1987 issue of *The Third Decade* mention is made of a November 22 1986 meeting of JFK critics in Dallas who viewed tapes relating to the Easterling claim. Other film was viewed including some footage taken by George and Jeanne De Mohrenschildt on a walking tour in Central America.

Robert Easterling's claim of being a low-level conspirator in the assassination of Kennedy was first publicised and examined in Henry Hurt's *Reasonable Doubt* (1986), Chapter 12, 'The Confession of Robert Easterling,' pps346-91. I know that most critics think Hurt was taken for a ride, but I have always thought that Easterling might have obtained some information secondhand from someone who was involved.

[140] LBJ: THE EARLY YEARS.

USA, MTV. 1986. Director: Peter Werner.
Color. Running time: 156 minutes.
CAST: Randy Quaid (LBJ), Patty LuPone (Ladybird), Morgan Brittany, Charles Frank, etc.

A lively and reasonably accurate dramatization of LBJ on the make-and-take covering the years from 1934 when he worked as an aide to a Texas congressman through to 1963 when he became President after the assassination.

[141] HOOVER VS. THE KENNEDYS [THE SECOND CIVIL WAR].

USA cable TV, 1987. Director: Mike O'Herlihy. USA/Canada coproduction.
Color. Running time: 180 minutes.
CAST: Robert Pine, Barry Morse, Heather Thomas (Marilyn Monroe), Richard Anderson, Jack Warden, Nicholas Campbell, etc.
A dramatization of the conflict between Hoover and the Kennedys taking in the civil rights demonstrations, wire-tapping, the mob and related issues. The assassination is also included.

[142] VIEWPOINT SPECIAL: The Men Who Killed Kennedy.

ITV, London. 25 October 1988. Producer/director: Nigel Turner.
Color. Running time: 125 minutes.
Not shown in USA until late September 1991 on Arts and Entertainment network.
[Note: Nigel Turner used this same title again for a three part documentary that

was shown in London on 20, 21 and 22 November 1991: see No. 167 below. The footage for the 1991 version is, essentially, the material shot during the making of the present program but not included here].

Producer-Director: Nigel Turner. Associate Producer: Susan Winter. Editor: Paul Jackson. Camera: Stephen McNutt, John Varnish. Camera Assistants: Bonnie Blake, Paul Rudge. Sound: Algis Kaupas, Vaughan Roberts, Robin Ward. Production Assistant: Louise Redfern. Graphics: Brian Becker. Dubbing Editor: Angela Davison. Research: Sheila Kogan, Jane Mercer, Janet Rayner. Narrator: Hilary Minster.

Archives: Agence France Presse, Antenne 2, Paris, British Broadcasting Corp., Columbia Broadcasting System, Sherman Grinberg, Independent Television News, JFK Library, Boston, KTVT-TV, Fort Worth, KXAS, Fort Worth, National Archives, Washington, National Broadcasting Company, UPI/Bettmann Newsphotos, Visnews, Worldwide Television News. Consultant: Matthew Smith [author of *JFK: The Second Plot* (1992)]. With Special thanks to: John E. Allen, Assassination Archives, Allied + WBS, Claire Alter, Belton Inn Family, Tom Dillard, Larry Harris, Paul Hoch, Conover Hunt, Bill and Gayle Newman, Gary Shaw, John Sigalos, Josiah Thompson. Senior Program Consultants: Robert Groden, Gary Mack. Photographic Consultants: Geoffrey Crawley, Jack White. Copyright Central Independent Television PLC 1988.

The Men Who Killed Kennedy can be divided into three sections. The first is a critical examination of the Warren *Report* with very good use of documentary footage and interviews, the second explores the discovery and implications of 'Badgeman' in the Mary Moorman photograph by Gary Mack and Jack White and includes interviews with two important and credible witnesses, Gordon Arnold and Ed Hoffman, while the third part examines Steve Rivele's allegations that three French petty criminals were the triggermen in Dealey Plaza - Saveur Pironti, Roger Bocognani and Lucien Sarti.

The source of Rivele's theory was Christian David, a drug smuggler and member of the 'French Connection' who was then serving time in Fort Leavenworth prison prior to being deported back to France and to whom Rivele had given legal assistance. Some hearsay substance was given to David's allegations by a Michel Nicoli, another drug smuggler and now a Federally-protected witness.

Rivele is the assassination's answer to P. T. Barnum. He appeared in front of the cameras claiming he had solved the case and had all the answers and he had nothing, merely heresay and surmise. There was nothing to substantiate his claims. Had his hypothesis been presented as that and nothing else there would have been no grounds for criticising the program's makers, but to present the documentary as the final answer to the puzzles of Dealey Plaza was an act of folly (see No. 146 for further comment on the French Connection).

Documentary footage includes: b&w of JFK at the Fort Worth Chamber of Commerce breakfast, leaving Fort Worth on Air Force One, color of the arrival at Dallas, sound footage of JFK's death being announced at Parkland, Parkland exteriors in color, Parkland corridors, casket being loaded on Air Force One, Andrews AFB unloading.

The Hughes and Nix films (Nos. 23 and 32) are shown together with the Zapruder film in an enhanced slowed version. There is good coverage of Dealey Plaza after the assassination and several TSBD exterior and interior shots.

The Tippit murder scene is shown soon after the shooting. B&w footage of the Texas Theater is included which appears to have been taken just after the arrest of Oswald. There is also a clip of what seems to be Oswald being driven into the Dallas PD after his arrest. Various shots of Oswald in police custody including a press conference. Ruby's slaying of Oswald shown. Ambulance leaving Dallas PD with Oswald, arrival at Parkland and Oswald being moved on a stretcher, and an announcement at the hospital: 'Mr. Oswald died at 1.07 our time in the operating room of the gunshot wound which he had received.'

Contemporary b&w footage is shown of the Tague curbstone being removed and Chief Curry at a press conference announcing (with an expression of resigned despair) that all of the police department's files on the assassination are being handed over to the FBI.

Warren Commission film includes several members of the Commission visiting Dealey Plaza, Earl Warren and Gerald Ford vignetted in a window of the TSBD, Allen Dulles being interviewed in Dealey Plaza, and Earl Warren himself visiting Jack Ruby in gaol. A final shot is of Warren handing his *Report* to LBJ in the White House.

The Men Who Killed Kennedy contains the most comprehensive selection of archival footage relating to Jack Ruby. Apart from the Oswald slaying there is b&w footage of Ruby going to court, of the judge giving the verdict and sentencing Ruby at the end of the trial, Ruby at a Dallas PD press conference, the Carousel Club, color shots of 'Jada' dancing, and an intriguing interview with Ruby by a journalist(?):

RUBY: Everything pertaining to what's happening has never come to the surface. The world will never know the true facts of what occurred...my motives. The people [inaudible] so much to gain and...and had such a material motive to put me in the position I'm in...will never let the true facts come...to the world.
JOURNALIST: Are these people in very high places, Jack?
RUBY: Yes.

Contemporary color footage is shown of Ruby's coffin leaving Parkland after his death and being flown back to Chicago.

New Ruby footage shot for the program includes Ruby's birthplace, a house on the West Side in Chicago, and the apartment he had in Dallas in a complex that resembles a seedy motel (complete with exterior shots of a filled-in swimming pool sprouting grass).

INTERVIEWS: Paul O'Connor, medical technician, Bethesda; Robert Groden; Gary Mack; Dr. Cyril H. Wecht; Governor John Connally; Senator Ralph Yarborough; Dr. Robert McClelland, Parkland; Dr. Paul Peters, Parkland; Aubrey Rike, ambulance/funeral home (interview includes period footage of him arriving at Parkland); Eugene Boone, Dallas PD; Paul Bentley, Dallas PD; Bob Carroll, Dallas PD; Gus Rose, Dallas PD; L. C. Graves, Dallas PD; Jim Leavelle, Dallas PD; Billy Grammar, Dallas PD (telephone threat against Oswald, probably from Ruby); Marilyn Sitzman, Abraham Zapruder's secretary; Phil Willis; Mrs. Phil Willis; Ms. Willis; Harold Weisberg; James Tague; Seth Kantor; Beverly Oliver, 'the babushka lady,' Dealey Plaza witness; Billy Bremmer, Dallas PD; Don Archer, Dallas PD; Mary Moorman, Dealey Plaza witness (period and new interviews); Jack White, photographic expert; Gordon Arnold, Grassy Knoll witness; Ed Hoffman, Dealey Plaza witness; Steve Rivele; Michel Nicoli, drug smuggler who alleged a French connection in the assassination; Fletcher Prouty.

The Rivele allegations and a rebuttal of Nigel Turner's documentary were the subject of a TV discussion program nearly a month later, No. 146.

Anthony Summers gives a detailed and more lenient account (than the present writer's) of the Rivele allegations in *The Kennedy Conspiracy* (1989), pps523-7. Jim Marrs' *Crossfire* (1989) contains a good account of Arnold's evidence and 'The Badgeman,' pps72-81, and a résumé of Ed Hoffman's eyewitness testimony, pps81-5.

This documentary was reviewed by Jan Stevens in 'A Video Compendium (Part Two)' in the September 1990 issue of *The Third Decade*.

[143] LATER: Dan Rather Interview.

NBC-TV, New York. 3 November 1988.
Color. Running time: 22 minutes.

An interview with Dan Rather on the *Later* program conducted by Bob Costas. Rather discusses his reconstructed memories of the Dallas assassination and the aftermath, his interviews with eyewitnesses, and the viewing of the Zapruder film. Rather stated at the time after seeing the Z-film that JFK's head was thrown forward! For further Rather see Nos. 144 and 169.

[144] THE JFK ASSASSINATION: 25 YEARS LATER.

CBS-TV, New York. 14-23 November 1988: 8 parts, 'Evening News.'
Color. Cumulative running time: 55 minutes.
Hosted by Dan Rather.

Rather-jaundiced examination of the controversies surrounding the
assassination.
    INTERVIEWS: Joseph Ball; David Belin; Arlen Specter; David Slawson; Dr.
Cyril H. Wecht; Jean Hill; G. Robert Blakey; John H. Davis; Priscilla
McMillan; Walter Cronkite; Jean Daniel, the journalist who questioned Castro
on the JFK assassination; Daniel Harker; John and Mrs. Nellie Connally;
Judith Exner; Ruth Paine; William Colby; Evelyn Lincoln; Jim Leavelle; Ed
Becker; Vincent Bugliosi; Rolando Cubella.

[145] NOVA: Who Shot President Kennedy?

PBS-TV, USA. 15 November 1988. Writer/producer/director: Robert Richter.
Color. Running time: 56 minutes.
Researcher: Steve Lyons. Narrator: Walter Cronkite.

As Jan Stevens has written (see below), despite its professional production
quality and gee-whiz computer graphics *Nova* was content to 'lean vaguely
toward the Warren Commission' findings. The principal areas examined are the
case against Oswald, the single bullet theory, the Grassy Knoll and
photographic evidence (including the Zapruder and Nix films, the latter not
credited, and the Moorman photograph), the accoustics evidence, and David
Lifton's body-change hypothesis.
    The partial version of the Zapruder film shown is widely regarded as the
most clear and color-accurate version in circulation, and did not come from
Robert Groden.
    Nova took four of the Parkland doctors - Drs. McClelland, Peters, Jenkins
and Dulany - to the National Archives to examine for the first time the 52
autopsy photographs. This had been arranged with special permission from the
Kennedy family. The doctors' reactions, by and large, were consistent with
what they 'remembered' from 1963...but were not consistent with what they *said*
in 1963. Their testimony is analysed in Stevens' article noted below.
    INTERVIEWS: Josiah Thompson, critic, author of *Six Seconds in Dallas*
(1967); David S. Lifton; G. Robert Blakey; Dr. Cyril H. Wecht; Darrell C.
Tomlinson, finder of the Magic Bullet at Parkland; Dr. Vincent P. Guinn,
ballistics expert, House Select Committee; Malcolm Summers, Grassy Knoll
witness; and the following Parkland doctors: Robert McClelland, Paul Peters,
Robert Shaw, James Jenkins and Richard Dulany (Governor Connally's

surgeon); Dr. Michael Baden; Bobby Hune; Louie Steven Witt, the supposed 'Umbrella Man' from House Select Committee footage; interviews with Paul O'Connor and Aubrey Rike taken from David Lifton's video, *Best Evidence*, No. 165.

For a full discussion of the program see Jan Stevens' 'PBS-TV's *Nova*: "Who Shot President Kennedy?": A Review' in *The Third Decade*, January 1989, pps3-11.

[146] VIEWPOINT 88: The Men Who Killed Kennedy - Discussion.

ITV, London. 16 November 1988.
Color. Running time: 25 minutes.
Production team: Mike Rossiter, Cherry Farrow, Peter de Selding, Vicki Marks, Nicki Ebenau, Louise Redfern. Facilities: Atlantic Video, Alexandria, Virginia. Videotape Editor: Ralph Cassano. Director: Hector Stewart. Producer: Nicholas Claxton. Copyright Central 1988.
Moderator: Peter Sissons.
PANELLISTS: Howard Willens - Warren Commission; Robert Groden; G. Robert Blakey; James Duffy; Nigel Turner.

This discussion program was produced by Central Television in response to the extravagant allegations made by Steve Rivele in Nigel Turner's *The Men Who Killed Kennedy*, No. 142. Rivele claimed that there were three French assassins in Dealey Plaza: Saveur Pironti, Roger Bocognani and Lucien Sarti. Rivele's source for the allegation? A French drug-runner in Fort Leavenworth, Christian David.

The program opens with clips from *The Men Who Killed Kennedy* and then proves through interviews and documentation that all three of the accused Frenchmen had alibis for 22 November 1963. Sarti was ill in hospital, Bocognani was in prison serving a sentence for buggery, while Pironti was doing his military service.

Nigel Turner did his best during the discussion to defend his position in the face of Sissons' emotive and hostile questioning (what a pity that Sissons can never quite muster the same aggression when questioning politicians), Howard Willens spoke like he had just stepped out of a 1963 time capsule, James Duffy said he would not be opposed to a new investigation, Robert Blakey was...well, just Robert Blakey, a figure who cannot understand how anyone could still have any questions left after *he* has investigated something. In the face of such company, Robert Groden was understandably taciturn.

INTERVIEWS: Maître Henri Juramy (Christian David's attorney); Sauveur Pironti, alleged assassin; Maître Jean-Claude Valera, attorney for Pironti; Jean-Louis Levreaux, editor of *Le Provençal*; Maître Marc Greco, attorney for Roger Bocognani.

A background piece on the program appeared in *The Sunday Times,* London, on 24 November 1991: 'Kennedy murder film attacked as a "TV lie"'.

[147] DISPATCHES: The Day the Dream Died.

Channel 4, London. 16 November 1988 (repeated 11 September 1989). Directors: Kevin Godley and Lol Creme.
Color. Running time: 42 minutes.
Production company: Exposed Films for Channel 4. Producer and presenter: Chris Plumley. Directors: (Kevin) Godley and (Lol) Creme. Executive producer: John Gaydon. Writer and program editor: Lino Ferrari. Editor: Jerry Chater. Lighting camera: Ernie Vincze. Sound: Albert Bailey. Art Director: Gerry Judah. Music: Buster Field, David Lazaro. Voice of the Warren Commission: Mark Smith.
Archive material: Associated Press, 'Best Evidence' courtesy of David S. Lifton, British Library, Dr. [*sic*] Abraham Zapruder, Colorific, Dr. H. John Gordon, Jacques Lowe, Jean-Michel Charlier, John Hillelson Agency, John F. Kennedy Library Foundation, Keystone Collection, KXAS-TV - Dallas/Fort Worth, Major Cecil Stoughton, National Archives - Washington, National Broadcasting Company, Okamoto Photos, *'Rush to Judgement'* film by Emile de Antonio and Mark Lane, Sherman Grinberg Film Libraries Inc., Sygma, Timo Mikkonen, WDSU[-TV] - New Orleans, Worldwide Television News.

The Day the Dream Died is a good hard-hitting documentary examination of the assassination that does not quite come up to its overly ambitious agenda. The chief questions it sets out to answer are: 1) Why was the casket empty at Andrews AFB? 2) What did LBJ gain from the assassination? 3) Who was the sniper in the Nix film (see below)? 4) Why did so many witnesses die? 5) How was it that Lee Harvey Oswald was arrested so quickly? 6) Who set Ruby up? 7) Why was JFK's body changed before the autopsy? 8) Why did the Dallas doctors change their views 'the very next day'? 9) Why was JFK's brain missing? 10) Why did the Warren Commission deceive the world? With so many major questions 42 minutes is cutting it a little fine for answers.
    In a graphically well presented sequence Chris Plumley argues that there were at least six shots fired in Dealey Plaza. These were: 1) The shot that struck somewhere near the Triple Underpass, a richochet from which grazed James Tague, 2) JFK's throat wound shot from the Grassy Knoll, 3) The shot fired from behind which hit JFK below the neck, 4) A shot fired at the same time as the preceeding which was the first hit Connally received, 5) The JFK head shot fired from the Grassy Knoll, 6) A shot fired from behind that hit Connally in the wrist.
    The Day the Dream Died utilizes contemporary newsreel material to good advantage and in addition to the use of the Zapruder and Nix films, discussed

below, includes footage as follows: the WDSU-TV interview with Oswald filmed on 21 August 1963 in New Orleans in which Oswald says 'I'm a Marxist' (this is No. 6 above), period color footage from New Orleans, New Orleans footage of Oswald distributing handbills with another unidentified individual (either No. 1 or 4), color of Air Force One leaving Fort Worth and arriving at Love Field, several color shots of the Kennedys and the Connallys, a b&w clip of Police Chief Jesse Curry saying 'I don't anticipate any violence', good coverage of the motorcade, amateur footage of the underpass and the Grassy Knoll immediately after the assassination including the famous shot of the police officer leaping from his bike and joining the crowds running up the Grassy Knoll, various color and b&w shots of the Texas School Book Depository including police officers entering the building, mute footage of Dr. Robert Shaw at Parkland (presumably announcing the condition of Connally), several shots of Oswald in police custody, Ruby in the background at the police press conference (a scene admirably re-created in *Ruby and Oswald*, No. 119), Marina and Marguerite Oswald, the ambulance and other vehicles travelling from Parkland to Love Field, and long, medium and close shots of Air Force One at Andrews AFB.

Part of Governor Connally's 1964 press conference is shown.

Some color footage of Jack Ruby in 1967 is included which has not to my knowledge been used in any other compilation. Ruby is walking down a corridor surrounded by police, lawyers and others. It was shot during his appeal. A journalist says something to Ruby and he turns to the camera:

RUBY: When I mentioned about Adlai Stevenson - if he was Vice President there would never have been an assassination of our beloved President Kennedy.
JOURNALIST: Would you explain it again?
RUBY: Well, the answer is the man in office now [ie LBJ].

Plumley adds that the woman who shot the film subsequently committed suicide.

There is also a contemporary newsreel interview with Police Chief Curry filmed, I believe, sometime on the Saturday which is worth transcribing:

JOURNALIST: Chief, did the FBI or your department have him [Oswald] under surveillance prior to yesterday?
CURRY: No, sir. We didn't have knowledge he was in the city.
JOURNALIST: Did the FBI?
CURRY: I understand they did know he was here and had interviewed him a week or two ago.

A few hours later Curry calls a press conference:

CURRY: I want to correct anything that might have been misinterpreted or misunderstood and that is regarding information that the FBI might have had about this man. I do not know if and when the FBI has interviewed this man. The FBI is under no obligation to come to us with any information concerning anyone. They have co-operated with us in the past one hundred per cent.

Some years later we discovered what had transpired to change the Police Chief's mind. FBI agent James Hosty had told the Dallas PD that the Bureau was aware of Oswald. This information resulted in Curry's first statement. After he had made it Gordon Shanklin, the FBI Special Agent-in-Charge in Dallas, Hosty's boss, telephoned Curry and told him that he must retract the statement, which he duly did. Shanklin subsequently denied making the call but then, in the words of Mandy Rice-Davies, he would, wouldn't he? See *The New York Times,* 2 September 1975, 'Dallas Ex-Police Chief Alleges an FBI Cover-Up on Oswald.'

A further interview with Curry has him saying that there are some 1200 men in the Dallas PD and that 'less than 50 men even knew Jack Ruby, and less than a dozen had ever been in his place of business' (why 'place of business'? Why not night-club?). In the documentary this is followed by Nancy Hamilton, a Ruby employee, flatly contradicting Curry and saying that there were very few officers who had not been in the club at sometime or other.

The program examines the single bullet theory in some detail with a full-scale mock-up of the Presidential limousine and there is a good presentation of the conflicts in the Dallas versus Bethseda medical evidence.

INTERVIEWS: James Tague; Bill Dodd; S. M. Holland; Nelson Delgado; Nancy Hamilton, taken from *Rush to Judgement,* No. 85; Aubrey Rike; Paul O'Connor; Jerrol Custer from *Best Evidence*, No. 165 (on the caption credits Rike's name is given as *Wright* and Jerrol Custer becomes *Gerald* Custer).

The Zapruder film is shown in the original and enhanced versions and in the latter synced with the Dictabelt sound recording.

The Orville Nix film too is shown in original and enhanced versions. The French film director Jean-Michel Charlier (see Nos. 107 and 108) obtained from Nix's son a copy of the film made before the original was handed over to the FBI and according to the program's narrator this is considerably different from the post-FBI version. Charlier's print was optically enhanced and enlarged and reveals very clearly a figure on the Grassy Knoll pointing a rifle at Kennedy.

There is no mistaking that what is shown is a rifleman but until details of just what enhancement steps were taken I suspend judgement on the issue. It is at this point that the sober and balanced tenor of the program goes out the window. The rifleman is alleged to be David Ferrie!

[148] JFK: AN UNSOLVED MURDER.

KRON-TV, San Francisco. 18 November 1988. Producer/writer: Stanhope Gould.
Color. Running time: 50 minutes.
Presenter: Sylvia Chase. Consultant: David S. Lifton.

INTERVIEWS: David S. Lifton; Josiah Thompson; Dr. Cyril H. Wecht; Robert Groden; Anthony Summers; John H. Davis; David Belin; Dr. Michael Baden, House Select Committee; Andrew Purdie, House Select Committee; Dennis David, Bethesda; Paul O'Connor; Floyd Riebe, Bethesda technician; Jerrol Custer; Aubrey Rike; Dr. Charles Carrico, Parkland; Dr. Ronald Jones, Parkland; Dr. Robert McClelland, Parkland; Dr. Marion Jenkins, Parkland; Nurse Audrey Bell, Parkland; John H. Davis; Burt Griffin, Warren Commission.
   Reviewed by Jan Stevens in 'A Video Compendium (Part Two)' in *The Third Decade,* September 1990.
   See Groden and Livingstone's *High Treason* (1989), pps386-402, and Livingstone's *High Treason 2* (1992), pps349-50.

[149] GERALDO: The Killing of JFK.

USA, TV. 22-23 November 1988.
Color. Running time: 90 minutes.

A two-part examination of the controversies presented by Geraldo Rivera. Part 1: Eyewitnesses to the Crime of the Century. Part 2: A Conspiracy of the Mob.
   INTERVIEWS: Dr. Cyril H. Wecht; David Belin; Jim Leavelle; Ed Becker; John Connally and Mrs. Connally; James Tague: Jean Hill; Jim Marrs; John H. Davis; David Scheim; Joe Cody, Dallas PD; Esther Mash, who claims she saw Ruby with Oswald at the Carousel; Madlyn Brown, LBJ's mistress.

[150] JFK: THAT DAY IN NOVEMBER.

NBC-TV, New York. 22 November 1988.

A memorial tribute to JFK hosted by Tom Brokaw that features interviews with many Kennedy aides. The assassination is recalled by the eye-witnesses noted below.
   INTERVIEWS: Charles Brehm; Jean Hill; Bobby Hargis.

[151] LARRY KING LIVE: JFK Discussion.

CNN-TV, USA. 22 November 1988.
Color. Running time: 35 minutes.
A discussion on the assassination.
    INTERVIEWS: David Belin; David Scheim; Gore Vidal.

[152] OPRAH WINFREY: The JFK Assassination.

USA TV syndicated. 22 November 1988.
Color. Running time: 45 minutes.
A chat show discussion on questions arising from the assassination.
    INTERVIEWS: Jean Hill; Earl Ruby, Jack's brother; Richard B. Stolley.

[153] AMERICAN EXPOSE: Who Murdered JFK?

USA TV. November 1988.
Color. Running time: 85 minutes.

An inquiry into the assassination conducted by the journalist Jack Anderson
who attempts to demonstrate that organised crime was largely responsible
(possibly with the aid of Castro).
    INTERVIEWS: Frank Sturgis; E. Howard Hunt; Marita Lorenz; Robert
Maheu; Bill Roemer, FBI agent on the wire tapping of Carlos Marcello; Dr.
Victor Weiss (on the Rose Cheramie incident); Pat Kirkwood; Mark Lane;
David Scheim; Dan Moldea; Gaeton Fonzi; John H. Davis; G. Robert Blakey;
Jean Hill; Malcolm Summers; Billy Grammar; Marina Oswald; Gerald R. Ford;
Melvin Belli; George McGovern; Ed Becker; Madlyn Brown; Esther Mash;
Gerry Hemming; Marina Oswald; Jean Hill.

[154] CHRONICLE: Best Evidence - The Magic Bullet and the Assassination
of JFK.

WCVB-TV, Boston. November 1988.
Color. Running time: 20 minutes.

An examination by the TV program *Chronicle* into the single bullet theory's
ballistic and accoustic evidence, presented by Mike Barnicle of the *Boston
Globe*.
    INTERVIEWS: Arlen Specter; Dr. Vincent DiMaio, who examined the disin-
terred body of Lee Harvey Oswald; Dr. Cyril H. Wecht; Robert Hunt, testing the
accuracy of the Mannlicher-Carcano rifle.

[155] EVENING NEWS: Who Shot JFK?

KPIX-TV, USA. November 1988.
Color. Running time: 20 minutes.
A program hosted by Josiah Thompson that examines three areas relating to the assassination: the evidence for a second gunman, Marina Oswald and her belief that her husband was a patsy, and the aftermath, concentrating chiefly on Jacqueline Kennedy.

[156] THE KWITNY REPORT: Mafia Involvement in the JFK Assassination?

USA TV syndicated. November 1988.
Color. Running time: 55 minutes.

Jonathan Kwitney's examination of mob involvment in the JFK assassination presented within an historical perspective that begins with the Estes Kefauver Hearings.
    INTERVIEWS: Aaron Kohn, New Orleans Crime Commission; Joe Nells, the Kefauver investigation; Ed Becker, on Carlos Marcello's threats against Kennedy; David Scheim; Dan Moldea; John H. Davis; Arlen Specter; David Belin; Victor Marchetti; Edwin Juan Lopez, House Select Committee attorney.

[157] NIGHTLINE: Was Oswald Shooting at Connally?

ABC-TV, New York. November 1988.
Color. Running time: 22 minutes.

A discussion on the *Nightline* program as to whether Oswald was actually trying to assassinate Governor Connally as proposed by the Connally biographer, James Reston, Jr.
    INTERVIEWS: James Reston, Jr.; Liz Smith; David Halberstam; John Connally.

[158] SUNDAY MORNING: A Remembrance of JFK.

CBS-TV, New York. November 1988.
Color. Running time: 55 minutes.
A 25th anniversary remembrance that includes amongst the hagiographic items Dan Rather recalling the scene in Dallas.

[159] REASONABLE DOUBT: THE SINGLE-BULLET THEORY AND THE ASSASSINATION OF JOHN F. KENNEDY.

USA. 1988. Director: Chip Selby.
Color. Video. Running time: 50 minutes.
Production company: CS Films Inc. Producer/editor: Chip Selby. Writers: Chip Selby, Mike Selby. Narrator: Mike Buchanan. Research consultants: Harold Weisberg, David [R.] Wrone. Assistant camera: Mike Selby, Sandy Svoboda [no credit is given for principal photographer, presumably Chip Selby?]. Assistant editor: Sandy Svoboda. Music: Steven Rosch.

Archive material: 20th Century Fox Movietonews, Ackad Studios, Forth Worth *Star-Telegram*, Sherman Grinberg Film Library, John F. Kennedy Library, KSAT-TV, National Archives, *The New York Times, Newsweek, US News and World Report, The Washington Post*, Harold Weisberg, WTN Corporation.

Thesis advisor: Dr. Gene S. Weiss. Special thanks: Department of Radio-TV-Film, University of Maryland, College Park.

Reasonable Doubt was produced as a doctoral thesis by Chip Selby while a student at the University of Maryland though one would never know that from the professional production values of the film. It is a superbly argued and well presented analysis of the single bullet theory and the surrounding medical evidence. The film won the Cine Golden Eagle Award for Outstanding Historical Documentary in 1988.

Footage of Kennedy's inaugural swearing-in and the funeral at Arlington, JFK coming out of the Texas Theater in Fort Worth, at Houston and San Antonio, Air Force One landing at Love Field (color), Dallas motorcade in color and b&w, Zapruder film in b&w, color and b&w shots at Parkland Hospital, two b&w clips taken at the scene of Tippit's murder with police cars and investigating officers (probably shot within an hour or so of the slaying), exterior footage of the Texas Theater in Dallas soon after Oswald's arrest, shots of Oswald in police custody including the famous confrontation with the press:

OSWALD: These people have given me a hearing without legal representation or anything.
QUESTION: Did you shoot the President?
OSWALD: I didn't shoot anybody. No, sir.

There are two TV clips of Ruby slaying Oswald: the low angle shot that also shows the confusion afterwards and a closer medium level that is freeze-framed when Oswald is hit.

Contemporary footage is also shown of Warren Commission members and Earl Warren, the famous scene at the Dallas PD when Oswald's rifle was held up for the press, Air Force One at Andrews AFB, and Governor John Connally's 28 September 1964 press conference at which he insisted he was hit by a different shot from the one that hit Kennedy.

Connally argued his case far better when being cross-examined by Arlen Specter for the Warren Commission: 'Well, in my judgement it just couldn't conceivably have been the first one because I heard the sound of the shot. In the first place, I don't know anything about the velocity of this particular bullet, but any rifle has a velocity that exceeds the speed of sound, and when I heard the sound of that first shot, that bullet had already reached where I was, or had reached that far, and after I heard that shot, I had the time to turn to my right, and start to turn to my left before I felt anything. It is not conceivable to me that I could have been hit by the first bullet, and then I felt the blow from something which was obviously a bullet, which I assumed was a bullet, and I never heard the second shot, didn't hear it.'

Also, remarkably, there are two mute movie clips of the famous Parkland doctors' press conference showing the White House aide Wayne Hawkes and Dr. Malcolm Perry in head-on and side angle shots, presumably taken by a local TV station.

INTERVIEWS: Dr. Cyril H. Wecht; Robert Groden (including talking over a stopped-frame version of the Zapruder film); Dr. Robert Shaw (Connally's surgeon at Parkland); Harold Weisberg; Professor David R. Wrone; Dr. Joseph Dolche (sp?).

Original video release in the USA. Commercially released in the UK on video by Castle Hendring/Castle Communications, 1990.

[160] THE LIFE AND LEGACY OF EARL WARREN.

PBS-TV, USA. October 1989.
Color. Running time: 88 minutes.

A documentary on the life and career of this celebrated US Supreme Court Justice. A good deal of attention is given to the Warren Commission, its methodology and findings.

INTERVIEWS: Joseph Ball; Arlen Specter; Gerald R. Ford; Jeffrey Earl Warren, who recalls conversations with his grandfather on the Commission, conspiracy theories, and alleged cover-ups.

[161] THE KENNEDY ASSASSINATION PHOTO CHRONOLOGY.

Quebec, Canada. 1989.
Color. Video. Running time: approx. 60 minutes.
Produced and released by Collector's Archives, Quebec.

The *Photo Chronology* is a video tape compilation of the still photographs taken in Dallas on 22 November 1963 starting with the arrival of Air Force One and covering the motorcade, the assassination, Parkland Hospital and after. All of the most famous stills are included.

Alphabetically, the photographers are:

Willie Allen, James Altgens, O. B. Ashmore, Jack Beers, Hugh Betzner, Wilma Bond, Richard Bothun, Henry Burrows, Henry Cabluck, Jerrold Cabluck, Frank Cancellare, Robert Croft, Gene Daniels, William Davis, Tom Dillard, Matt Herron, Shel Hershorn, Bob Jackson, Joe Laird, Jim MacCammon, Joe McAulay, David Miller, Dan Moorman, Mary Moorman, Jim Murray, Justin Newman, James Powell, Stuart Reed, Art Rickerby, Flip Schulke, Walt Sisco, George Smith, Cecil Stoughton, Jim Towner, Al Volkland, Jack Weaver, E. H. Westfall, Lewis Williams, Phil Willis.

Frames from motion picture footage are used for continuity and the films included are:

Tom Atkins, F. M. Bell, Charles Bronson, Malcolm Couch, Jack Daniel, Elsie Dorman, Robert Hughes, John Martin, Charles Mentesana, Mary Muchmore, Orville Nix, Patsy Paschall, Tina Towner, David Weigman, Abraham Zapruder.

[162] FAKE.

Dallas, Texas. September 1990. Director: Jim Marrs.
Color. Video. Running time: 49 minutes.
Executive Producers: VJS Companies, Jack White. Producer: Perry Tong. Associate Producer: Pat Tong. Script: Jim Marrs (adapted from research by Jack White). Production: Third Coast Productions. Editor: Tharon Henderson. Camera: Dan Suggs, Kevin Morris. Audio: Michael Bandy. Still photography: Kyle Tong. Graphics: James Aden. Music: Manhattan. Rifle and camera courtesy of the JFK Assassination Information Center, Dallas, Texas.

Anchorman: Craig Maurer. Reporter: Dan Foster. Interviewee: Jack White. In film re-creation: Don Istook as Oswald, Tracy Millhollan as Marina.

Copyright JFK Video Group 1990. Obtainable from JFK Video, 301 West Vickery, Fort Worth, Texas 76104.

This is one of the most compelling documentaries arising from the JFK assassination. It is the result of Jack White's 25 years investigation into the famous Oswald 'backyard' photographs taken in Neely Street, Warren Commission Exhibits 133-A and 133-B, showing Oswald holding the Mannlicher-Carcano rifle and a folded copy of the Communist newspaper, *Militant*.

Through White's research the film demonstrates beyond any doubt that the pictures were faked, possibly before the assassination. There is extensive use of blow-ups, comparisons and overlays, and of the possible techniques employed in fabricating the pictures. This is also the film for cinema buffs who get off on the dark-room sequence in Antonioni's *Blow Up.*

There is also discussion of a further Neely Street picture that was found amongst Roscoe White's effects in 1976, then in the possession of his widow (here dubbed Exhibit 133-C), and of the photograph that George de Mohrenschildt kept which is similar to 133-A but with more detail.

What appears to be part of the 'smoking gun' in the faking of the picture was the discovery in early 1992 amongst the Dallas PD papers of a photograph of the Neely Street backyard with the area occupied by Oswald masked-out (see No. 171). Further discussion by Jack White of the photo appears in No. 168.

[163] RUNNING AGAINST TIME.

USA TV. 21 November 1990. Director: Bruce Seth Green.
Color. Running time: 120 minutes.
Production company: Finnegan-Pinchuk Productions in association with MCA TV Entertainment. Executive Producers: Pat Finnegan, Sheldon Pinchuk. Co-executive producer: Michael Weisbarth. Producer: David Roessell. Screenplay: Robert Glass and Stanley Shapiro, based upon Shapiro's novel, *A Time to Remember.* Photography: Brian Hebb. Music: Don Davis. Editor: Heather MacDougall. Production designer: Barry Robinson.
CAST: Robert Hays (David Rhodes), Catherine Hicks (Laura Whittaker), Sam Wanamaker (Dr. Koopman), James DiStefano (Lee Harvey Oswald), Brian Smiar (Lyndon B. Johnson), etc.

A university history professor, David Rhodes, cannot escape from his brother's tragic death in Vietnam some 25 years earlier. Rhodes meets Dr. Koopman on the campus who is engaged in secret research into time travel. Rhodes persuades Koopman to send him back to Dealey Plaza on 22 November 1963 figuring that if he can prevent Oswald from shooting Kennedy the Vietnam war will be avoided and his brother's life saved. But things go wrong. Rhodes arrives on the roof of the Texas School Book Depository and cannot get to Oswald in time. Kennedy is shot and Rhodes is arrested for the crime. Laura is subsequently sent back to rescue him but nothing goes according to plan....

The late Stanley Shapiro's 1986 novel, *A Time to Remember,* was a time travel romp that was distinguished by some touching and elegant writing, even if it lacked the scientific 'nuts and bolts' exegesis that this minor literary genre needs if it is to be credible. But the cracks in the story that Shapiro's deft prose could paper over are thrown into sharp relief by the poor production values and hurried approach of the film. The best moments are the performances of

DiStefano as Oswald and Smiar as LBJ. The rest is pretty forgetable.

The film, like the book, takes on board uncritically the view of the Warren *Report* that Oswald was the sole assassin. In this respect it seems to hark back to the balmy, immediate post-*Report* days of the 1960s when such acceptance was widespread. A view that seems distinctly out of place in a work dating from the mid-1980s.

The idea that if Kennedy had not been assassinated there would have been no Vietnam war is, of course, also the basis of Oliver Stone's *JFK*, No. 225.

In the UK *Running Against Time* was not shown on TV or released theatrically. It went straight on to video sell-thru and was released by CIC in October 1991.

[164] 1963: A YEAR TO REMEMBER.

London. 1990.
B&w. Video. Running time: 57 minutes.
Production company: Parkfield Publishing, London, 1990. British Pathe News Library Director: George Marshall. Script: Jerome Vincent. [Series and Introductory] Narrator: Mark Roman. Original production work: First Frame Productions. Producer: Ray Glenister. Associate Producer: Paul Feldman. Executive producer: Michele Kimeche.

'All materials used in this video are solely derived from The British Pathe News Library, owned by the Parkfield Group plc.' Marketed and distributed by Parkfield Entertainment: A Division of Parkfield Group plc.

One of a series of commercially available video compilations based on the Pathe newreel and spanning the years 1930 through 1969. The 'President Assassinated' Pathe feature shown in British cinemas in late November, early December 1963 and discussed above at No. 68 is included here in its entirety.

Other items in the compilation showing JFK are the award of honorary US citizenship to Winston Churchill in April 1963 and footage of JFK's visit to England in June 1963 for talks with Prime Minister Macmillan. This latter item has some significant shots in the light of what happened five months later. Kennedy was staying with Macmillan at his large country house down in the country. On a Sunday JFK went to Mass at the Chapel of Our Lady of the Forest in Forest Row, a village near Macmillan's home. JFK is shown leaving the Chapel in an American stretch limo with a full overhead protective glass bubble, undoubtedly bullet-proof. Why the Secret Service believed that the small, deserted lanes of Sussex warranted such measures being taken while none were needed at Dealey Plaza is a mystery. This prompts the question: Has anyone researched the incidence of open-topped versus close-topped public appearances by Kennedy during his presidential years?

[165] BEST EVIDENCE: THE RESEARCH VIDEO.

Santa Monica, California. 1990. Executive producer: David S. Lifton.
Color. Video. Running time: 36 minutes.
Co-Producers: Mark Dichter, David S. Lifton, Arnon Mishkin. Editor: Arnon
Mishkin. Sound: Mark Dichter. Camera: David Watts. Negative cutter: Larry
Mischel. Special thanks to: Jeremiah Kaplan, Albert Litewka, George Walsh.
   Wrap-Around Segments. Executive Producer: Richard Foos. Associate Pro-
ducer: Arny Schorr. Producer: David S. Lifton. Writer: David S. Lifton.
Photography: David Starrs. Editors: David Starrs, Jim Sevin. Lighting: Pedro
S. Padua. Music: David Starrs. Special thanks to: Tom Horton, Tom Horton,
Jr., Patricia Lambert, Ginger Liebovitz, Pat Valentino.
   Willis slides courtesy of Phil Willis. Copyright 1964-2039 [sic].
Inauguration and funeral sequences: Thomas Horton Associates from *America
Remembers John F. Kennedy.* Headsnap sketches: J. Simon Design. Additional
graphics: US National Archives, JFK Library, LBJ Library, Cecil Stoughton.
Autopsy photographs courtesy of Mark Crouch. Original source: James K. Fox,
US Secret Service.
   Best Evidence: The Research Video - Copyright 1980, 1990; RPPL, Inc.
'Direct Inquiries to: David S. Lifton, c/o Rhino Home Video, 2225 Colorado
Avenue, Santa Monica, CA 90404.'

Best Evidence is a documentary video pendant to Lifton's 1980 book of the
same name which seeks to establish that somewhere between Love Field and
Bethesda Kennedy's body was removed from the casket and clandestinely
altered prior to the autopsy at Bethesda Naval Hospital. Thus the evidence of
the body (the 'best evidence') would then show, after alteration, that Kennedy
was shot by a single assassin from behind.
   The film includes documentary footage of Air Force One arriving at Love
Field, Dallas motorcade clips, stills from Dealey Plaza and footage of the
Grassy Knoll immediately after the assassination, numerous exterior shots
taken at Parkland Memorial Hospital, and library footage of the casket being
taken from Air Force One at Andrews AFB ('6.00pm EST'). Also included are
several of the JFK autopsy photographs that Lifton obtained in 1981 from
James K. Fox, a retired officer of the Intelligence Division of the US Secret
Service (seven of them are included in the 1988 edition of Lifton's book).
   INTERVIEWS: Dennis David, Chief of the Day at Bethesda; Aubrey Rike, fu-
neral attendant, Dallas; Paul O'Connor, Medical Technician, Bethesda; Jerrol
Custer, X-ray Technician, Bethesda.
   Lifton's documentary discusses the type of casket used, the Dallas versus
Bethesda evidence, the arrival of the caskets at Bethesda, the body bag, and the
Sibert/O'Neill FBI report.
   The film was originally shot in 1980 (see No. 120) prior to the initial

publication of Lifton's book, *Best Evidence*, and, according to a flyer at the back of the 1988 Carroll and Graf edition, had a running time of 23 minutes. The present version has an additional running time of 13 minutes which comprises the wrap-around segments of Lifton introducing and discussing his findings.

The copy I viewed was commercially released in the UK in February 1992 by PolyGram Video Ltd in the wake of Oliver Stone's movie, *JFK*, and, indeed, the front wrapper gives the appearance that the title is 'JFK' rather than *Best Evidence*.

See the two editions of Lifton's book (1980 and 1988) and for dissenting views: pps423-8 of Henry Hurt's *Reasonable Doubt* (1986) and Harrison Livingstone's article 'Concerning David Lifton and "Best Evidence"' in the January 1987 issue of *The Third Decade*.

The Willis slides that Lifton makes good use of are discussed by Harold Weisberg in *Whitewash II* (1966), pps 229-41.

[166] THE THIRD DECADE RESEARCH CONFERENCE.

Fredonia, New York. 28-30 June 1991. Director: Eduardo Rosario.
Video.

The Conference was held at Fredonia State College, NY, on 28-30 June 1991 and was organised by Jerry D. Rose, editor and publisher of *The Third Decade* magazine. Eduardo Rosario videotaped the papers given at the Conference and these are available from Jerry D. Rose on a personal loan basis (as are copies of the papers themselves). Inquiries to: Jerry D. Rose, *The Third Decade*, State University College, Fredonia, New York 10463, USA.

The following papers were presented:

THE SINGLE SHOT TO THE PRESIDENT'S HEAD: Robert Cutler.
    Discussant: Nick Bartetzko.
GREER, ZAPRUDER AND THE 'SMOKING BULLET': Vincent Palamara.
    Discussant: Robert Cutler.
BELIN'S BOMBSHELL: G. J. Rowell. Discussant: Charles Drago.
THE USE OF COMPUTERS IN RESEARCHING THE ASSASSINATION OF
    PRESIDENT KENNEDY: Anthony Marsh. Discussant: Joseph Hamilton.
LOVE FIELD: George Michael Evica. Discussant: Martin Shackelford.
THE MAN WHO HEARD TOO MUCH: AN UPDATE: Peter Whitmey.
    Discussant: Bill Rudd.
THE MAFIA, THE CIA, OR BOTH? CONTENDING CONSPIRACY
    THEORIES IN THE JFK ASSASSINATION CASE: John H. Davis.
THE BODY ALTERATION THEORY AND PARKLAND HOSPITAL: Joel
    Wagoner. Discussant: Harrison Livingstone.

ASSASSINATION FICTION: ITS IMPACT UPON AND VALUE TO THE
INVESTIGATION OF THE ASSASSINATION OF PRESIDENT KENNEDY:
   Charles Drago. Discussant: Andrew Winiarczyk.
WHAT WE KNOW ABOUT THE JFK ASSASSINATION: Jerry D. Rose.
THE FUTURE OF THE THIRD DECADE: Panel, chaired by George Michael
   Evica.

Note: Vincent Palamara in his paper noted above showed an improved,
enhanced version of the Zapruder film that 'possibly shows a bullet in flight'
just before the Z-313 headshot.

[167] THE MEN WHO KILLED KENNEDY.

Thames Television, London. 20, 21 and 22 November 1991.
Producer/director: Nigel Turner.
Color. Running time (total): 252 minutes.
Three part documentary first transmitted by Thames Television, London, on 20
November (The Cover-Up), 21 November (The Patsy), and 22 November (The
Witnesses) 1991.
[For Nigel Turner's earlier documentary of the same title and from which the
present film is derived see No. 142).
Associate Producer: Susan Winter. Editor: Paul Jackson. Camera: Stephen Mc-
Nutt, John Varnish. Sound: Algis Kaupas, Vaughan Roberts, Robin Ward.
Graphics: Brian Becker. Narrator: Hilary Minster. Senior Program Consultants:
Robert Groden, Gary Mack.
   Archives: British Broadcasting Corporation; Columbia Broadcasting
System; Sherman Grinberg; JFK Library, Boston; KTVT-TV, Fort Worth;
KXAS, Fort Worth; National Archives, Washington; National Broadcasting
Company; Visnews; Worldwide Television News. With Special Thanks to:
John E. Allen; Assassination Archives; Allied + WBS; Belton Inn Family; Dan
Christensen; Roy Cooper; Geoffrey Crawley; Tom Dillard; Paul Hoch; Conover
Hunt; S. Monitor; Marina Porter; Michael Weigall; Jack White.
   Copyright Central Independent Television, 1989.
The credits remain the same for the three parts except that the name Clare
Alter is added to the 'With Special Thanks' section of Parts 2 and 3.
THE COVER-UP (Part 1). Running time: 50 minutes.
THE PATSY (Part 2). Running time: 50 minutes.
THE WITNESSES (Part 3). Running time: 52 minutes.

The three parts explore nearly all of the major questions raised by the critics
and in a telling and sympathetic manner. Turner, by letting the witnesses and
critics speak for themselves, has produced one of the best documentary studies
(all references to the theories of Steve Rivele have been dropped, *vide* No. 142).

See Groden and Livingstone's *High Treason* (1989), pps389-402.

Part 1: THE COVER-UP

Good detailed discussion and analysis of Dealey Plaza, the medical evidence (subscribing to the Lifton thesis), the missing brain, the three tramps, Jack Ruby, just how Ruby gained access to the basement, and the taping of Joseph Milteer in Miami (including a long interview with Everett Kay (sp?) of the Miami PD, the officer in charge, and a transcription of the Milteer/Willie Somersett tapes).

Good contemporary color and b&w footage of Dallas motorcade, activity in Dealey Plaza immediately after the assassination including good coverage of the TSBD outside and inside (officers on the sixth floor), newsreel footage of 'The Cellar' in Fort Worth (where the Secret Service spent the night before the assassination), color and b&w of Parkland and the drive to Love Field, Andrews AFB (including LBJ's statement), Oswald slaying, various Dallas PD interiors. Comprehensive coverage of funeral in Washington including JFK's lying in state.

Mute color shots of Ruby in courtroom.

The Zapruder and Nix films are shown in original and enhanced versions.

Good new footage was especially shot for the documentary in and around Dallas, at Walter Reed and Bethesda hospitals, and outside and in Oswald's apartment on Neely Street in Dallas (where FBI Agent Hosty first interviewed Marina).

INTERVIEWS: James Hosty, FBI; Robert Groden; Gary Mack; Gary Shaw; Bill and Gayle Newman (together with 1963 Dealey Plaza footage); Mary E. Woodward; Fletcher Prouty; Bobby Hargis, Dallas PD; Luke Mooney, Dallas PD; Ralph Yarborough; Dr. Paul Peters; Aubrey Rike; Paul O'Connor (an original interview, not from *Best Evidence*, No. 165); Dr. Cyril H. Wecht; Charles Harrelson (in prison); Seth Kantor; Roy Vaughn, Dallas PD; Larry Harris; Patrick Dean, Dallas PD; Everett Kay(sp?), Miami PD.

Part 2: THE PATSY

The second part explores Oswald's life in Dallas prior to the assassination, the Tippit slaying in detail, Oswald's arrest and death. His period in New Orleans is also examined and there is an interview with Jim Garrison together with interviews in Jackson regarding Oswald's sheep-dipping. The subject of who was actually buried (and disinterred) in Oswald's coffin is explored and there is some startling testimony from Paul Groody. Period footage of TSBD interiors and exteriors, Texas Theater, Oswald in Dallas police custody, interview with Chief Curry, burial of Tippit, and burial of Oswald.

The WDSU-TV 16 August 1963 footage of Oswald distributing leaflets outside the New Orleans Trade Mart is included as is the 21 August interview with Oswald in which he claims to be a Marxist (Nos. 4 and 5 above).

New footage of the Oak Cliff, North Beckley, and Irving neighborhoods of Dallas is included, as is the Tippitt slaying locale. There are also many shots of

New Orleans and a trip out to Jackson.

There is good coverage of the 1981 disinterment of Oswald and Dr. Linda Norton, the pathologist, is shown reporting the results of her examination at a press conference.

INTERVIEWS: Robert Groden; Ruth Paine; Buell Wesley Frazier; Harold Norman, TSBD employee; Marion Baker, Dallas PD; Helen Markham (filmed at Tippit scene); Ted Callaway, Tippit witness; Larry Harris; Butch Burroughs; Gerald L. 'Gerry' Hill, Dallas PD; Jim Leavelle, Dallas PD; Gus Rose, Dallas PD; Dr. Paul Peters, Parkland; Paul Groody, Miller's Funeral Home; Gary Mack; Jim Garrison; Adrian T. Alba; Edward Lee McGehee, barber from Jackson (see James Kirkwood's *American Grotesque* [1970], pps213-5, for his testimony in the Shaw trial); Reeves Turner, State Representative, Jackson.

Part 3: THE WITNESSES

Interviews with some of the Dealey Plaza witnesses, the Parkland doctors, and officers of the Dallas PD. Following the death of JFK the arrest and examination of Oswald is explored and the circumstances surrounding his slaying, this in some detail. Oswald and the trip to Mexico City are discussed. The Parkland versus Bethesda medical examination is presented. And after a brief discussion of the Dictabelt and the acoustical evidence the question of who benefited from the assassination is argued.

Good contemporary color footage of the motorcade. B&w footage of Oswald in police custody including two versions of the slaying. Father Hubert at Parkland. Shots of Marguerite and Marina at Parkland. The Zapruder film in original and enhanced versions.

INTERVIEWS: Beverly Oliver; Phil Willis, Mrs. Phil Willis and Ms. Willis; Mary E. Woodward; Dr. Robert McClelland; Dr. Paul Peters; Aubrey Rike; Bob Carroll, Dallas PD; Gerald Hill, Dallas PD; Gus Rose, Dallas PD; Ruth Paine; Jim Leavelle, Dallas PD; James Hosty; Larry Harris; L. C. Graves, Dallas PD; Patrick Dean, Dallas PD; Dan Archer, Dallas PD; Paul O'Connor; Dr. Cyril H. Wecht; Robert Groden; Gary Mack; Harold Weisberg; Ralph Yarborough.

The Men Who Killed Kennedy was commercially released on video in the UK in September 1992 by PolyGram Video.

[168] THE MANY FACES OF LEE HARVEY OSWALD.

Fort Worth, Texas. December 1991. Writer/director: Jim Marrs.
Color. Video. Running time: 59 minutes.
Executive Producers: Jack White, Pat Tong. Producer: Perry Tong. Editor: Tharon Henderson. Videography: Douglas Mugby. Audio: Third Coast Studio, Joe Turner, On Track Video. Re-enactments director: Perry Tong. Music: Manhattan. Graphics: Third Coast Productions. Lighting and Set Design: Douglas Mugby. Research and Photo-Analyst: Jack White. Special thanks to the JFK

Assassination Information Center for Oswald rifle and Roscoe White photos.

Anchor: Craig Maurer. Commentator: Jim Marrs. Special Reporter: Dan Foster.

RE-ENACTMENT CAST: Don Istook (Lee Harvey Oswald and impersonators), Gale Metcalf (FBI Agent 1), Jim Hunter (FBI Agent 2), Janette Nave (Sylvia Odio), Lori Ann Larson (Marina Oswald), Jack Young (Garland Slack), Bobby Perkins (Oscar Deslatte), etc.

Copyright JFK Videos and Third Coast Productions 1991. Released February 1992. Obtainable from JFK Video, 301 West Vickery, Fort Worth, Texas 76104.

This is a follow up to *Fake*, No. 162, again written and directed by Jim Marrs and featuring Jack White's compelling research.

White discusses further the famous backyard photograph of Oswald taken in Neely Street and shows how, based on the size of the communist newspaper Oswald is holding, his height in the photograph is only 4ft 11ins! White goes on to discuss Roscoe White and his belief that Roscoe was the body-double for Oswald in this photograph (Jack White's detailed analysis of the photographs is in *Fake*, No. 162).

There is a detailed examination of Oswald's life and his intelligence connections and many little known photographs are used. Jack White analyses many of the photos of Oswald to argue that a substitution was made for the real Oswald *after* he left the Marines but *before* he went to Russia, and it was this substitute who returned from Russia and was arrested for the assassination (unlike Michael Eddowes who argues that the switch was made in Russia, by Russians using a Russian). The subject of the 'second' Oswald is examined in some depth and is dramatized using actors. The exhumation is also discussed and White argues that the Oswald exhumed in 1981 appears not to have had a craniotomy, whereas Oswald was subjected to the procedure in the 1963 autopsy.

[169] CBS NEWS: 48 HOURS: JFK.

CBS-TV, New York. 5 February 1992.
Color. Running time: 56 minutes.
Presenter: Dan Rather. Reporters: Phil Jones, Erin Moriarty, Richard Schlesinger.

Executive Producer: Andrew Heyward. Director: Alan Shapiro. Producer (*sic*): Liza McGuirk. Producers (*sic*): Nancy Duffy, Jonathan Klein, Linda Martin, Mary Murphy, Bernard Birnbaum, Rand Morrison. Associate Producer: Claude Becker. Writer: Thomas Flynn. Associate Director: Ron Flaum. Coordinating Editor: Joan Turturro. Camera: Roberto Alvarez (and 11 others). Sound: Juan Caldera (and 12 others). Researchers: Mary Ellen Noonan, Joseph Young.

Post Production Editor: Mark J. Oberthaler. Music: Edd Kalehoff. Special thanks to: Leslie Midgley [Midgley was the producer of the 1967 CBS documentary, No. 84 above].

Zapruder Film: Copyright 1967 & 1963 LMH Co, c/o James Silverberg, Esq. Washington DC. 202.332.7978. All rights reserved.

For a transcript send $4.00 to Journal Graphics, 1535 Grant Street, Denver, CO 80203.

Dan Rather has always had a special place in the critics' demonology since he announced after a private screening of the Zapruder film ,soon after the assassination, that it showed Kennedy's head being thrust *forward* ('Nearly right, Mr. Rather!'), an announcement he subsequently admitted was wrong.

Here we have Rather 'building on more than 28 years of reporting' attempting to shore up the Warren *Report* while graciously admitting, as a sop to the critics, that there may be things we will never know (not that they effect the main contentions of the *Report,* you understand). The program is a sorry mix of misunderstanding, misinformation and evasion that can be best summed up by its reaction to the question as to whether the CIA was responsible for JFK's death? No, says Rather. His evidence? Richard Schlesinger holding a microphone in front of Richard Helms and asking him if the Company was responsible. No, says Helms, certainly not. And thus the word of a proven liar is enough for the guys at CBS.

Nevertheless, this edition of *48 Hours* is valuable for the period footage and interviews: JFK at the Fort Worth breakfast, the Hughes and Zapruder films, good footage of the motorcade and of Dealey Plaza immediately after the assassination including numerous exteriors of the TSBD, the Tippit scene, the Texas Theater, and a very good selection of shots of Oswald in police custody and footage of Ruby at a Dallas PD press conference. Further material includes the Oswald slaying, Parkland hospital, Walter Cronkite announcing JFK's death in the famous 1963 television newsflash, the Ruth Paine house in 1963, and a pan of the Warren Commission and, from some years later, the House Select Committee in session.

An extended biographical section on Oswald has clips from three of the films shot in New Orleans: the WDSU-TV 16 August 1963 film of Oswald alone handing out leaflets in front of the Trade Mart, (No. 4), the 21 August interview made by the same TV station (No. 6), and a further leaflet distribution shot that may be either the Doyle film (No. 1) or the WWL-TV footage (No. 5).

A section on the Garrison investigation includes a rare clip of Clay Shaw denying his guilt in a prepared press statement. His precise and clipped ennunciation sounds more Boston than New Orleans and if you were to close your eyes you would think he was British (for Clay Shaw's English connections see the present writer's *Late-Breaking News on Clay Shaw's United Kingdom*

Contacts [1992]).

The program concludes with a lengthy section on Oliver Stone's *JFK* that includes an interview with Stone and several clips from the film.

INTERVIEWS: Period footage of numerous unidentified Dealey Plaza witnesses. Harold Norman and James E. Jarman, Jr. Period interviews with: Howard L. Brennan, Dealey Plaza witness; Cecil J. McWatters, Oswald bus driver; William Whaley, Oswald cab driver; Helen Markham, Tippit shooting; Ted Callaway, Tippit shooting; Johnny Brewer, shoe shop manager; Police Chief Jesse Curry; Marguerite Oswald; Marina Oswald; Ruth Paine; Clay Shaw.

New interviews: Robert Tannenbaum, House Select Committee attorney; David Belin, Warren Commission; Dr. Cyril H. Wecht; John Connally; Henry Wade; Carl Day, Dallas, PD; Jim Leavelle, Dallas PD (interviewed in basement of police station); Mac Osborne, Oswald room-mate; William Colby; Richard Snyder, US consul in Moscow at time of Oswald defection; Ed Hoffman; Mark Lane; Michael L. Kurtz (author of *The Crime of the Century* [1982]); Richard Helms; Lyndon Johnson, 1969 interview with Walter Cronkite alleging 'international connections' in the assassination (No. 100); Jonathan Kwitny; Oliver Stone.

[170] CHANNEL 2 LOCAL RESPONSE: New York Area.

CBS-TV/Channel 2, New York. 5 February 1992.
Color. Running time: 3.5 minutes.
Presenter: Ernie Anastos.

After the showing of the *48 Hours* documentary above Channel 2 broadcast a three minute 'local response' that included color footage of the 1969 Walter Cronkite interview with Lyndon Johnson in which LBJ says that there were 'international connections' in the JFK assassination. Johnson asked that this section of the interview not to be shown at the time, citing 'national security.'

Anastos interviews Cronkite who now admits that it is 'hard not to think there was a conspiracy.'

The 'local response' is rounded out with some vox pop interviews in the wake of the release of Oliver Stone's *JFK*.

[171] THE DALLAS POLICE JFK FILES.

Fort Worth, Texas. March 1992. Writer/presenter: Jim Marrs.
Color. Video. Running time: 9 minutes.
Presenter: Jim Marrs. Executive Producers: Perry Tong, Jack White. Director: Ron Youngblood. Editor: Tharon Henderson. Camera operators: Douglas Magby, Bill Crossland. Associate Producer: Jim Allen.

Copyright Third Coast Productions and JFK Videos 1992. Released in March 1992. Obtainable from JFK Video, 301 West Vickery, Fort Worth, Texas 76104. Produced as a 'teaser' for a forthcoming Jim Marrs video.

Early in 1992 the City Council of Dallas voted to release all of the Dallas police files held on the JFK assassination. Jim Marrs, the author of *Crossfire* (1989), who has taught a JFK assassination course at the University of Texas, Arlington, since 1976 was one of the first researchers to examine the papers and in this 9 minute video he discusses some of the more intriguing findings.

Documents reveal that four hitherto unknown witnesses testified to seeing Ruby with Oswald prior to the assassination including a man who claimed he drove David Ferrie and Oswald to Ruby's club.

A report says that only *two* 6.5mm cartridges were found in the TSBD, while the results of a paraffin test on Oswald's face proved negative - he had not fired a rifle that day.

Particularly intriguing was the discovery of a photographic print of Oswald's Neely Street backyard with Oswald's shape masked-out in white. This would appear to be an intermediate stage in the faking of the famous backyard photo of Oswald holding a rifle, Commission Exhibit 133-A (see Jack White, No. 162).

Marrs also shows the arrest reports on the famous 'Three Tramps' and asks how it is that the Warren Commission and the House Select Committee could not discover them despite repeated searches, and, indeed, why the Dallas PD denied having them, yet here they are? The alleged tramps are named as Harold Doyle, John Forrester Gedney and Gus W. Abrams. Who they are if, indeed, they actually exist is a question still to be answered. The report sheets are tantalizingly free of any facts beyond their ages, Doyle was 32, Gedney 38, and Abrams an old-timer at 53, *and* Doyle's home address in Red Jacket, West Virginia. Gedney and Abrams have the word 'None' entered under HOME ADDRESS (the reports are reproduced in Livingstone's *High Treason 2* [1992] on pps609-11).

See Michael Canfield's 'The Cover-Up Continues' in *Dateline Dallas* (Dallas), Summer/Fall 1992, for some intriguing investigations into Doyle, including a curtailed interview. I do not think we have heard the last of the Three Tramps.

[172] BEYOND JFK: THE QUESTION OF CONSPIRACY.

USA. July 1992. Producer/director: Danny Schechter.
Color. Video. Running time: 90 minutes.
Video release by Globalvision.

[173] FAKE.

USA. July 1992.
A national re-release by 3G Video Productions of No. 162, unchanged except
that the narration is now done by G. Robert Blakey.

[174] THE JFK ASSASSINATION: THE JIM GARRISON TAPES.

USA. July, 1992. Directed by John Barbour.
Color. Video. Running time: 90 minutes.
Blue Ridge/Film Trust presentation: A John Barbour Film. Writer, director:
John Barbour. Executive producer: Tom Kuhn. Coexecutive producer: Lamar
Card. Producer: Fred Weintraub. Coproducer: Sarita Barbour. Supervising
producer: Steve Jaffe. Camera: Greg Bader, Dennis P. Boni, Steve Elkins,
Robert Perrin. Supervising editor: Ronald D. Burdett. Sound design and effects:
Michael Wetherwax. Video engineer: Tom Kemp. Audio engineer: Mike
Mannion. Music: David Wheatley. New Orleans consultant: Steve Tyler.
Research consultants: Fred Newcomb, Mary Ferrell, Gary Mack, Steve Jaffe.
    Archival Films and Photographs courtesy of: The John F. Kennedy Library,
National Archives, Garrison Family, NBC News, Gary Mack, Chip Selby,
Mark and Tricia Lane, Blackstar Pictures, Chrisita Corporation, Harold
Weisberg, Jim Lezar [sic], the Assassination Research Center, Washington DC,
Steve Jaffe.
    Additional thanks to: Dallas Police Department, New Orleans District
Attorney's Office, Visitor's Television (VTV), New Orleans, Gayle Nix
Jackson, the Garrison Family.
    Zapruder film copyright 1967 and 1963 LMH Company c/o James Lorin
Silverberg Esq, Washington DC (202) 332.7978.
    Nix film copyright Orville Nix Family.
    JFK Productions Inc copyright 1992. Vestron Video/Live Distributing Inc.

A comprehensive and wide-ranging presentation of Jim Garrison's case through
interviews with and voice-overs by New Orleans' most illustrious District Attorney. The video examines the personal background of Garrison and the origins
and progress of his investigation into the JFK assassination and the subsequent
trial of Clay Shaw. The documentary also explores more general questions
relating to the assassination such as the CIA's involvement, the Milteer tape
recording, number of shots, the backyard photo of Oswald, Oswald and
Lovelady, the medical evidence, the magic bullet, David Ferrie, and the House
Select Committee.
    Contemporay newsreel footage includes: Oswald in New Orleans
distributing leaflets alone, with another, and the TV interview (Nos. 4, 5 and
6), JFK at Love Field, color and b&w footage of the motorcade in Dallas,

Dealey Plaza post-assassination scenes including police inside the TSBD, Tippit scene of crime newsreel, exterior Texas Theater, Parkland Hospital exteriors, Malcolm Kilduff at the Parkland Hospital press conference announcing JFK's death (with sound), Oswald in police custody, Henry Wade, Ruby slaying Oswald, Ruby in custody and at trial, Governor Connally press conference, excerpt from the Universal Newsreel on 'The Warren Commission.' And from the Garrison investigation, Clay Shaw alone and with his attorneys, Garrison press conferences and trial scenes, Dean Andrews,

INTERVIEWS: Jim Garrison; Nicholas Katzenbach, former Deputy Attorney General; Bill Alford, Garrison's Assistant DA; Fletcher Prouty; Dr. Robert McLelland, Parkland Hospital; Ed Hoffman, Dealey Plaza eye-witness, interpreted by his daughter, Mary Hoffman Sawyer; Jim Leavelle, Dallas PD; Steven Jaffe, Garrison's photo-analyst; Jim Marrs; Harold Weisberg; Robert Groden; Gayle Nix Jackson, on the disgraceful interviewing of Orville Nix by CBS for the June 1967 TV documentary, No. 84 above; Mark Lane; Lou Ivon, Garrison's chief investigator; Perry Russo, now a New Orleans cabdriver, an impressive witness; F. Irvin Dymond, Clay Shaw's counsel; Elizabeth, Eberhardt and Virginia Garrison, Jim Garrison's children; Gary Mack.

LIBRARY INTERVIEWS: David Atlee Phillips, former chief of the CIA's Western Hemisphere Division; Roger Craig, Dallas PD; J. C. Price, Orville Nix, S. M. Holland, James Leon Simmons, Richard C. Dodd, Lee Bowers, and Mary Moorman from Mark Lane and Emil de Antonio's film, *Rush to Judgement* (No. 85); Bill Newman and Jean Hill, from contemporay local Dallas TV; Jesse Curry; Gordon Shanklin, Dallas FBI chief; Dean Andrews and Walter Sheridan from NBC's *The JFK Conspiracy: The Case of Jim Garrison* (No. 83); Jim Garrison, from his right-of-reply response to the NBC documentary, No. 86.

The Zapruder film is shown several times in slowed down and enhanced versions and with the synced sound of the Dictabelt recording. The version shown in the latter half of the documentary is easily the sharpest and clearest I have ever seen. Good versions are also shown of the Nix, Hughes and Bronson films.

Released on video in the UK by Braveworld, August 1992.

[175] THE MARK OAKES INTERVIEWS.

St Louis, Missouri. October 1992. Producer/director: Mark Oakes.
Color. Video. Running time: 277 minutes.
Interviewer, producer, director, camera: Mark Oakes. Assistant: Stan Szerszen.

Mark Oakes, virtually alone in the critical community, has in the last couple of years been diligently video-taping witnesses who either have not been interviewed before or, if they have, encouraging them to talk at greater length than interviewers with commercial considerations. Oakes' relaxed and discursive interviewing style allows the subjects time to open-up and digress. They are not being pressurized for sound-bites.

Oakes is performing a valuable service not just for the community but also for posterity and I hope his example encourages others to do the same. Twenty years ago filming interviews was an expensive and time consuming business, but now with the video recorder supplanting motion picture technology more researchers should be out in the field taping people before it is too late.

Oakes can supply the interview tape in whole or in part together with transcripts and related documents including newspaper cuttings and FBI reports. Contact him at 10346 Briar Hollow Drive, Apt. #6, St Louis, Mo. 63146, USA.

INTERVIEWS: J.W. Foster, Dallas PD, the uniformed patrolman in the famous sequence of photographs taken on 22 November in Dealey Plaza showing him with Deputy Sheriff Buddy Walthers examining a bullet on the grass which was then taken away by an FBI(?) officer and never seen again; Bill and Gayle Newman, Dealey Plaza witnesses; Malcolm Summers, the Dealey Plaza witness who believes shots came from the Grassy Knoll and who had a curious encounter with a speeding car on Houston Street immediately after the assassination; Mr. and Mrs. Wayne Hartman, Dealey Plaza witnesses who confirm the furrow in the grass observed by Walthers and Foster (in addition to interviewing them at home, Oakes also takes them back to Dealey Plaza where they show the exact location of the furrow, not far from where Jean Hill was standing); Al Maddox, Dallas PD, who was with Buddy Walthers when he was killed by a felon in 1969; Beverly Oliver; Jim Leavelle, Dallas PD; D. V. Harkness, Dallas PD, on the epileptic seizure in Dealey Plaza, the arresting of the Three Tramps, and his Warren Commission testimony; Roy Vaughn, Dallas PD, who was stationed at the top of the ramp at the Dallas police headquarters on Sunday 24 November and who was unfairly and erroneously blamed by the Warren Commission for allowing Jack Ruby to slip past him; Charles Brehm, Dealey Plaza witness; Henry Wade, Dallas DA.

[176] ASSASSINS!/ASSASSINATIONS.

USA. 1992. Writer/producer/director: Nick Bougas.
Color. Video. Running time: 53 minutes.
A Screen Entertainment Production. Executive producer: Ray Atherton. Associate Producers: F. B. Vincinzo, Charles Miller. Narration: Harold Wells. Music: Peter H. Gilmore, George Montalba. Editor: Gordon Pepper. Sound: Terry Corliss. Special Photography: John Leiberman.

Film clips courtesy of: Golden West Film, Encore News, Kreklow Film, Vintage Video, Madhouse Video, Southbank Film, TLC Communications, Classic Clip Collections.

Copyright Wavelength Productions 1992. Released in the UK in May 1992 by Screen Entertainment/Murderers [*sic*].

This is a cheaply produced, as opposed to low budget, video in a series entitled *Murderers, Mobsters and Madmen* that appears to be aimed at the crowd who chase gruesome murderers and serial killers. The tape is titled *Assassins!* but the UK cover, over a photograph of JFK, prints *Assassinations.* One wonders if the companies who release these videos ever actually look at the product.

The first eight minutes explore the history of assassination in general and American political asassinations in particular (prior to JFK) in the manner that the subject might be treated by *True Detective* magazine. Included here is newsreel footage of the first assassination captured on movie film - the murder of King Alexander 1st of Yugoslavia in Marseilles in 1934.

An eight minute section then recounts the assassination of JFK and this is put together more professionally than the rest of the documentary.

Some rare stills of Oswald are included that I had not seen before. There is a clip of Oswald distributing leaflets in New Orleans with the unidentified colleague (No. 5), the Zapruder and Nix films in whole and part, various angles of the motorcade, and quite the most extensive footage of Parkland exteriors and interiors included in any compilation, including a shot of what appears to be Trauma Room One. There are several Dealey Plaza and TSBD clips that show the scene immediately after the assassination, and also good coverage of the Tippit murder scene.

The usual footage of Oswald in police custody is included together with newsreel interviews with Jesse Curry and Henry Wade. The famous clip of Ruby standing with journalists at the Wade news conference is also shown.

Assassins! also uses the longest 'take' of the Oswald slaying I have seen. The camera holds on the scene after the slaying and includes Oswald being put on a stretcher, loaded on an ambulance and being driven off up the ramp. The soundtrack throughout this is a 'live' news-reporter, presumably from one of the local Dallas TV stations.

Other material includes Ruby in police custody, JFK family footage and the state funeral in Washington.

Harold Wells in his *March of Time*-style narration describes Oswald as an 'emotionally disturbed' child who later would possess a 'murderous nature,' and says that while controversy would continue to surround the assassination 'no hard evidence' would ever be found to dent the Warren Commission's conclusions (!).

After the JFK section film clips are shown of the two attempted assassinations of Gerald Ford (by Squeaky Fromme and by Sarah-Jane Moore), John Hinckley Jr.'s attempted shooting of Ronald Reagan, and Arthur Bremmer's wounding of Governor Wallace. The Bobby Kennedy and Martin Luther King slayings are also covered but, of course, not shown.

The last half of the tape dwells on the likes of Gary Gilmore, William Perry and Dick Smith.

[177] THE SEARCH FOR THE TRUTH.

Dallas, Texas. 1992. Producer/director: David Daugherty.
Color. Video. Running time: 50 minutes.
Independent Video Services present a JFK Assassination Information Center production. Writer: Bill Willbourn. Narrator: Kelly Burly. Production: New Age Video. Post Production: Independent Video Services. *Search for the Truth* lyrics and music by David D. Sung by Mark Chase. Sign interpreter for Ed Hoffman: Allison Randolph.
     Copyright 1992 Independent Video Services.

A well produced and informative promotional video for the JFK Assassination Information Center in Dallas that includes interviews with co-directors Larry Howard and Robert Johnston. There is good topographical footage exploring Dealey Plaza and other locations associated with Oswald and the assassination. Larry Howard discusses the Warren *Report* theories and presents the evidence for a gunman in the Grassy Knoll area that includes witness Ed Hoffman's re-enactment of what he saw on 22 November 1963. There is also a lengthy excerpt from a Howard lecture in which he recounts Ricky Don White's appearing at the Center claiming that his father, Roscoe White, was one of the gunmen in Dealey Plaza and what the Center subsequently uncovered about this mysterious figure. The 'mysterious deaths' of witnesses are also examined.
     INTERVIEWS: Larry Howard and Robert Johnston of the JFK Assassination Information Center; Madlyn Brown, LBJ's mistress for many years; Ed Hoffman, witness to a gunman on the Grassy Knoll; Aubrey Rike, ambulanceman, discussing the epileptic seizure in Dealey Plaza and later events at Parkland.
     This video is available directly from the JFK Assassination Information Center in Dallas (address in Introduction).

[178] THE ASSASSINATION OF JFK.
USA. 1992. Producer: Dennis Mueller.
Color. Video. Running time: 78 minutes.
Released by MPI Home Video.

[179] THE MIND OF L. FLETCHER PROUTY (MR. X IDENTIFIES GEN-
     ERAL Y).
USA. 1992. Producer: Brian Guig.
Color. Video. Running time: 60 minutes.
Video release by Prevailing Winds Research, Santa Barbara.

6

Collector's Archives Videos

Presented here are compilation and other videos offered for sale by Collector's Archives that did not readily fit into any of the other sections.

The V-numbers are ordering numbers and should be quoted in any correspondence with the company.

The entries are arranged in chronological order with undated items at the beginning. All material is sourced from the USA.

Collector's Archives: Box 2, Beaconsfield, Quebec H9W 5T6, Canada.

[180] ASSASSINS AMONG US.

No date given.
Color. Running time: 60 minutes.
V-034.
A documentary tracing the assassination and attempted assassination of Amercan political figures. Covers JFK, Bobby Kennedy, Martin Luther King, George Wallace, Gerald Ford, and Ronald Reagan. Original film included. Narrated by James Whitmore.

[181] GREAT FIGURES IN HISTORY: JOHN F. KENNEDY.

No date given.
Color. Running time: 100 minutes.
V-009.
A tribute to JFK originally released by CBS News in their *Collector's Series*. The video also includes *The Presidential Years* and *The Childhood Years*, two general interest JFK documentaries.

[182] G. ROBERT BLAKEY INTERVIEWS.

Compilation covering June 1979 to October 1981.
Color. Running time: 80 minutes.
V-071.
Interviews with the Chief Counsel of the House Select Committee taken from
ABC's *Good Morning, America,* PBS' *MacNeill-Lehrer Report,* NBC's *Tomorrow,* and KTVT-TV in Dallas. Blakey talks about the Select Committee, his
book, *The Plot to Kill the President* (1981), and Mob involvement in the
assassination.

[183] NBC-TV ANTHONY SUMMERS INTERVIEW.

NBC-TV, New York. 1980.
Color. Running time: 30 Minutes.
V-012.
NBC *Tomorrow* program interview by Tom Snyder with Anthony Summers
about his book *Conspiracy* (1980).

[184] ANTHONY SUMMERS INTERVIEWS.

1980.
Color. Running time: 65 minutes.
V-072.
Interviews with Anthony Summers discussing the assassination and the House
Select Committee from the following US TV programs: WFAA's *Saturday,*
KDFW's *Crossroads,* and KXAS' *Charlie Rose in Dallas.* Summers also talks
about his book *Conspiracy* (1980).
    Also included on the tape are filmed interviews done by Summers with Delphine Roberts and Antonio Veciana.

[185] DAVID LIFTON INTERVIEWS.

1981.
Color. Running time: 100 minutes.
V-070.
David S. Lifton on the campaign trail for *Best Evidence* (1980) discussing the
two casket theory on some five US TV programs.

[186] ENCORE NEWS: JFK FEATURE.

1982.
B&w? Running time: ?

V-073.
A retrospective look at Kennedy's Dallas trip that includes much period footage.

This also includes the Marguerite Oswald interview from the WFAA-TV program in 1978, No. 116.

[187] J. EDGAR HOOVER.

1982.
Color. Running time: 60 minutes.
V-015.
An investigative report from ABC News' *Close-Up* program critically detailing the life and times of Hoover. Some of the subjects covered are the vendetta against the Kennedys, the COINTELPRO program, Martin Luther King, and Lee Harvey Oswald.

[188] JFK: THEN AND NOW.

1983.
Color. Running time: 30 minutes.
V-024.
Dan Rather CBS *Evening News* reports on the assassination and the aftermath.
INTERVIEWS: Walter Cronkite; William Manchester; Frank Church; Gerald R. Ford.

[189] AIR FORCE ONE: THE PLANES AND THE PRESIDENTS.

1984.
Color. Running time: 60 minutes.
V-076.
A history of US presidential planes. Covers the assassination of JFK and the subsequent swearing-in on Air Force One of LBJ. Narrated by James Stewart.

[190] CBS-TV: THIS MORNING - REMEMBERING JOHN F. KENNEDY.

CBS-TV, New York. 14-22 November 1988.
Color. Running time: 70 minutes.
V-186.
CBS-TV's seven part (mini-)series on the 25th anniversary of the assassination, broadcast between 14 and 22 November 1988. Hosted by Harry Smith and Kathleen Sullivan.

Largely hagiographic. Many Kennedy aides and friends are interviewed.

A segment on assassination theories includes...

INTERVIEWS: Paul L. Hoch; Robert Blakey; Arlen Specter.

[191] THE GRASSY KNOLL GAZETTE: ASSASSINATIONS REVIEWED.

Continental Cablevision. 1988.
Color. Running time: 170 minutes.
V-212.
A six part series from Continental Cablevision's *The Grassy Knoll Gazette* hosted by R. B. Cutler. Cutler discusses his Umbrella Man theories, JFK conspiracy theories, the Martin Luther King shooting, Chappaquiddick, the Reagan attempted assassination and other matters.

Also included is a filmed interview with James Earl Ray by William Saussy, publisher of Ray's autobiography, *Tennessee Waltz.*

[192] MORTON DOWNEY JR. SHOW: THE LEGACY OF JOHN F.
    KENNEDY.

November 1988.
Color. Running time: 46 minutes.
V-183.
Downey discusses JFK's Vietnam policy, the CIA/Castro murder plots, JFK and the Mob, and other topics.

INTERVIEWS: Warren Hinckle; Carl Oglesby; Richard N. Goodwin, JFK speechwriter; Sidney Zion; Dotson Radar; Fred Otash, on wire-tapping JFK and Marilyn Monroe.

[193] RUBY - OSWALD: THE MURDER WITH 60 MILLION WITNESSES.

November 1988.
Color. Running time: 45 minutes.
V-179.
A segment from the syndicated series *Crimes of the Century* dealing with JFK and Oswald. Hosted by Mike Connors.

INTERVIEWS: Jim Garrison; Mark Lane; Seth Kantor; Melvin Belli; Abe Weinstein (owner of a rival nightclub in Dallas); Jim Leavelle; Earl Ruby, Jack's brother; Lavada Greer, Carousel Club employee; Rabbi Hillel Silverman, on Ruby's confession; Jerry Coley, with Ruby at the *Dallas Morning News* at the time of the assassination.

[194] SNIPER'S NEST DISCOVERED AT SITE OF JFK SHOOTING.

1988 (1991?).
Color. Running time: 15 minutes.

V-213.

A video 'walking tour' of Dealey Plaza made by Kenneth and James Collier. Includes shots of a supposed sniper's nest behind a sewer grating on the Grassy Knoll and a 'bullet scar' on an Elm Street curbstone.

The brothers Collier are probably better known for 'Votescam,' the name they have given to the alleged rigging of *all* US political elections by the News Election Service in New York. See Jonathan Vankin's *Conspiracies, Cover-Ups and Crimes: From JFK to the CIA Terrorist Connection* (New York: Dell, 1992), pps22-38.

[195] USA TODAY PROGRAM: OPENING OF TSBD ASSASSINATION
    MUSEUM.

20 February 1989.
Color. Running time: 25 minutes.
V-187.

A news segment by the syndicated US TV program, *USA Today,* covering the opening of the sixth floor of the TSBD as an exhibit in the JFK Assassination Museum.

Includes a discussion of JFK conspiracy theories with...

INTERVIEWS: Phil Willis; Bill and Gayle Newman; Jean Hill; David Belin; James Reston, Jr.; John Connally; Jim Leavelle; David S. Lifton.

[196] JACK RUBY'S GUN - HOLLYWOOD AND THE MOB.

CNN. December 1989.
Color. Running time: 20 minutes.
V-236.

News items broadcast by CNN on the legal tussle surrounding the ownership of Jack Ruby's effects (including the gun that shot Oswald).

INTERVIEWS: Earl Ruby; Jules Mayer, sometime Jack Ruby attorney.

This video also includes a section from the CBS *60 Minutes* examination of Hollywood and the Mob broadcast in November 1989 describing the Mob's connection with the entertainment industry (especially MCA).

7

Four(?) Films in the Life
of Lee Harvey Oswald

[197] WE WERE STRANGERS.

USA, 1949.
Directed by John Huston.
Columbia Films and Horizon Productions (S.P.Eagle [ie Sam Spiegel] and John
Huston). Photography: Russell Metty. Screenplay: John Huston and Peter
Viertel, from an episode in the novel *Rough Sketch* by Robert Sylvester. Editor:
Al Clark. Music: George Antheil.
CAST: John Garfield (Tony Fenner), Jennifer Jones (China Valdes), Pedro Ar-
mendariz (Armando Ariete), Gilbert Roland (Guillermo), Ramon Novarro
(Chief), etc.
B&w. Running time: 105 minutes.

Cuba in the early 1930s is dominated by a brutally repressive government.
China Valdes sees her brother murdered by the chief of the secret police and
then decides to avenge his death by joining the underground opposition. Tony
Fenner, an American revolutionary, conceives a daring plan to rid Cuba of its tyrann
by tunneling from China's house to the family tomb of an important politician in
a nearby cemetery and planting a bomb. After the bomb is planted the politician
is assassinated. The conspirators wait for the state funeral to be held at the
tomb so that all of the government can be blown up together, but then at the
last moment the funeral is held elsewhere. Fenner realises he has to escape and
after a shoot-out with the police he dies in China's arms as the first sounds of a
popular uprising can be heard in the streets outside.
  Variety, 27 April 1949, thought that in *We Were Strangers* John Huston 'has
come up with a finished job of directing that edges close to his best films.'

Huston went on to direct a lot better films and I think one would be hard pushed to find even a Huston devotee who would get enthusiastic about this production. The film's real interest are the good performances by Garfield and, to a lesser extent, Jones. The political and social background is not convincing and merely serves as a flimsy backdrop to the foreground melodrama. The story was based upon the overthrow of the Machado dictatorship in 1933.

On Saturday, 19 October 1963, the day after Oswald's last birthday, his 24th, he and Marina stayed up late and watched two films on a television double-bill according to Priscilla Johnson McMillan in *Marina and Lee* (1977), p380. These were *We Were Strangers* and *Suddenly* (following). McMillan writes: 'Marina remembers the movie's end - people were dancing in the streets, screaming with happiness because the president had been overthrown. Lee said it was exactly the way it had once happened in Cuba. It was the only time he showed any interest in Cuba after his return from Mexico.'

Gary Mack's researches show in fact that *We Were Strangers* was broadcast not on 19 October but on 13 October 1963, a Sunday, at 1.00pm and certainly not as a double-bill with *Suddenly*.

See further discussion under *Suddenly* below.

[198] SUDDENLY.

USA, 1954.
Directed by Lewis Allen.
A Robert Bassler Production. Script: Richard Sale. Photography: Charles Clarke. Editor: John Schreyer. Art Director: Frank Sylos. Music: David Raksin. A Robert Bassler Production. Distributed by United Artists.
CAST: Frank Sinatra (John Baron), Sterling Hayden (Tod Shaw), James Gleason (Pop Benson), Nancy Gates (Ellen Benson), Kim Charney (Pidge), James Lilburn (Jud), Clark Howatt (Haggerty), etc.
B&w. Running time: 75 minutes.

The Bensons live in the small Californian town of Suddenly. On the day that the President of the United States is due to alight from the presidential train (Rail Car One?) at Suddenly and drive out for a few days' fishing the Benson home is invaded by three gunmen led by John Baron (Frank Sinatra). The three hitmen have been hired to assassinate the President and they plan to execute him as he leaves the train from a window in the Benson house overlooking the station. In the event the train doesn't stop at Sudddenly after all and in an ensuing shoot-out Baron is shot dead by the local sheriff.

As noted under *We Were Strangers* above, Priscilla Johnson McMillan in *Marina and Lee* (1977), p380, claims that Marina and Oswald stayed up late on the night of Saturday, 19 October 1963 to watch a TV double-bill comprising the John Huston film and *Suddenly*. There was no such double-bill and *We*

Were Strangers was actually shown some days earlier. According to Gary Mack after an exhaustive search of contemporary TV listings, *Suddenly* was shown nowhere in the Dallas area between 13 and 26 October 1963. This is not to say that Oswald did not see the movie at some other time but it certainly brings into doubt McMillan's reliability as reporter.

The interest in *Suddenly* does not, however, end there. The film is intriguing for a number of reasons aside from the fact that it is about a presidential assassination. Sinatra plays a lone, mentally unbalanced ex-serviceman. He spent time as a kid in an orphanage. He has ties to organised crime. He learns how to kill in the army. He discusses the advantages of a high-powered rifle in an assassination. He intends to shoot from a window high above the president. These co-incidences and similarities are explored in Martin Shackelford's provocative article, 'Frank Sinatra's Assassination Role: Telling It Like It Wasn't,' in *The Third Decade,* September 1985.

In the wake of JFK's death *Suddenly* was withdrawn from distribution and was unavailable for many years. It has recently been released on video in the USA and UK (by 7th Art, May 1992).

Sinatra, it will be remembered, was for a time close to JFK and it was he who introduced Judith Campbell Exner to both Kennedy and Sam Giancana, but that's another story....

[199] BATTLE CRY.

USA, 1954.
Directed by Raoul Walsh.
A Warner Bros. Production. Photography: Sid Hickox. Editor: William Ziegler. Script: Leon Uris, from his novel *War Cry.* Art Director: John Beckman. Music: Max Steiner. Sound: Francis J. Scheid. Technical adviser: Col. H. P. (Jim) Crowe. Distributed by Warner Bros.
CAST: Van Heflin (Major Huxley), Aldo Ray (Andy), Nancy Olson (Pat), James Whitmore (Sgt. Mae), Raymond Massey (General Snipes), Tab Hunter (Danny), Dorothy Malone (Elaine), etc.
Warnercolor. CinemaScope. Running time: 136 minutes.

'Amatory, rather than military, action is the mainstay of this saga of the United States Marines,' commented *Variety* in its review of the movie, 2 February 1955, and that about sums it up. It is a sprawling World War Two epic scripted by Leon Uris and based upon one of his own interminable novels that charts the lives and loves of a group of youngsters in the Marine Corps from enlistment and basic training through to action in the Pacific. Ably directed by the veteran Hollywood action director, Raoul Walsh.

Battle Cry and *War is Hell*, following, were the double bill playing at the Texas Theater, 231 West Jefferson Boulevard, Dallas, on 22 November 1963 when Oswald was arrested. He was picked up 10 minutes after he arrived at about 1.50pm while watching *War is Hell* and thus did not have an opportunity of comparing his time in the Marine Corps with that presented by Uris and Walsh.

[200] WAR IS HELL [aka WAR HERO and WAR MADNESS].

USA, 1960.
Directed by Burt Topper.
Producer/director/screenplay: Burt Topper. Associate producer: Sam Altonian.
Photography: Jacques R. Marquette. Editor: Ace Herman. Music: Ronald Stein.
Burt Topper Productions.
CAST: Tony Russel, Baynes Barron, Judy Dan, Wally Campo, Bobby Byles, Tony Rich, Michael Bell, etc.
B&w. Running time: 75 minutes.

A cowardly sergeant is determined he must return from the Korean War a hero. His mad ambition drives him to kill an officer, claim that dead colleagues were cowards and continue fighting the war after the armistice has been signed. Later he undergoes a change of heart and lays down his life for his comrades.

   This and *Battle Cry* above comprised the double bill playing at the Texas Theater, 231 West Jefferson Boulevard, Dallas, on 22 November 1963 when Lee Harvey Oswald was arrested. Oswald was grabbed at about 1.50pm some 10 minutes after he arrived during the showing of *War is Hell*.

   Audie Murphy's name is often billed as the star of *War is Hell*, but in fact Murphy does not act or appear in the film, he merely supplies the opening off-screen narration.

   The title *War is Hell* was also used for a 16mm short directed by Robert Nelson and William Allen (USA, 1968).

8

Theatrical Motion Pictures

In chronological order. All films are 35mm in original release unless otherwise stated.

THE REAL NIGHTMARE ON ELM STREET

I have not transcribed all credits for the theatrical motion pictures listed below. This would have been time and space consuming and such information is more of interest to film students than assassination researchers (the credits for Oliver Stone's *JFK*, for instance, run to nearly 350 names) and, besides, it is readily available in publications such as the *Monthly Film Bulletin, Variety,* and similar. I have included the main credits, producer, lighting cameraman, editor and so on (see further the note under References, below), and then creamed the cast list. Other than that I have selected what I think will be of interest to JFK researchers - technical advisers, helpers, and so on. And this has thrown up a few surprises. Who now remembers that David Lifton and Penn Jones, Jnr., for example, were listed amongst the Technical Consultants on *Executive Action*?

The films dealt with here relate directly to or were inspired by the JFK assassination and thus I have excluded several pictures that are often seen by some as being relevant. Amongst these I would mention two fine films by John Frankenheimer, *The Manchurian Candidate* (1962) dealing with a programed presidential assassin and which may be more germane to Bobby Kennedy's assassination, and *Seven Days in May* (1964) about, essentially, the army and nuclear policies (in the same way that Stanley Kubrick's *Dr. Strangelove* might similarly be described!) and thus not concerned with the assassination, and one film by Martin Scorcese, *Taxi Driver* (1976), which several writers have claimed is 'also essentially about the Kennedy assassination' (the quote is from Jefferson Morley in the *Los Angeles Times,* 8 December 1991, but several other writers have said it too). True, Travis Bickel, the taxi driver of the title is an ex-marine and true, he does stalk a political candidate, but his attempted assassination is thwarted by the Secret Service and he then turns his homicidal frenzy to the young prostitute's pimp and customers. Woolly-thinking sociologists and journalists writing op-ed pieces can make tenuous connections but I do not think *Taxi Driver* belongs in the present list.

Finally, perhaps, I should mention Brian De Palma's *Blow Out* (1981) as Collector's Archives have frequently listed it as being of JFK interest. The story is about a candidate for political office who has a car tire blown out by a sniper-assassin, the car then plunges into a river. John Travolta plays a film sound technician who has recorded the incident and manages to save the politician's girlfriend but not the politician. Later he finds that his tapes reveal the sound of a gunshot. The reader may judge the relevance to the JFK assassination. Completists should note, however, that there is one passing reference to the Zapruder film.

And on the subject of De Palma I think a critic could argue that his career is a decline from a very good first film, through progressively worse and worse films. That first film is *Greetings* (1966, No. 204) and has a strong JFK assassination interest. It is discussed below.

Lastly, there are many films that mention the assassination en passant. I have included two only below, largely because of their humor, *Annie Hall* and *Full Metal Jacket*. But a note should be made here of Philip Kaufman's moving and impressive film about teenage gang members in the Bronx in 1963, *The Wanderers* (1979). The assassination is presented via the news shown on TVs in a shop window. A small crowd gathers. The times are changing. Deftly and poignantly done.

I have cross-referenced here the more important theatrical TV productions that are cataloged in part 5.

[201] DR. STRANGELOVE, OR HOW I LEARNED TO STOP WORRYING
AND LOVE THE BOMB.

UK/USA, 1963.
Directed by Stanley Kubrick.
Produced by Stanley Kubrick. Associate Producer: Victor Lyndon. Screenplay: Stanley Kubrick, Terry Southern and Peter George, based upon George's novel, *Red Alert*. Photography: Gilbert Taylor. Editor: Anthony Harvey. Music: Laurie Johnson. Columbia Pictures.
CAST: Peter Sellers (Group Captain Lionel Mandrake, President Muffley, Dr. Strangelove), George C. Scott (General Buck Turgidson), Sterling Hayden (General Jack D. Ripper), Slim Pickens (Major T. J. 'King' Kong), etc.
B&w. Running time: 94 minutes.

Stanley Kubrick's masterpiece has nothing to do with the JFK assassination but it was the first major film to be directly effected by the events in Dallas and it is noted here for that reason.

Jack D. Ripper, a psychotic US Army general, has ordered a nuclear attack on Russia. Major Kong in a B52 gets the 'go code' and proceeds to his target inside the USSR. Kong checks through the contents of the survival kits issued to the airmen (dollars, gold, roubles, prophylactics, a phrase book, etc) and comments, 'Shoot! A fella could have a pretty good weekend in *Vegas* with that stuff!'

Dr. Strangelove opened in New York on 3 December 1963, not quite two weeks after the assassination. When Kubrick originally shot the scene with Major Kong the dialogue recorded was 'A fella could have a pretty good weekend in *Dallas...*' but this was changed with an over-dub because of the assassination.

[202] EAT YOUR MAKEUP.

USA, 1966.
Directed by John Waters.
Produced, photographed, edited by John Waters.
CAST: Howard Gruber (JFK), Divine (Jackie Kennedy), etc.
B&w. 16mm. Running time: 40 minutes.

According to John Waters in *Premier* magazine (May 1992), 'I just wanted to go on the record that Divine was the first person ever to portray Jackie Kennedy on the screen.' Divine did so in this home movie that tells the story of a mad governess who kidnaps models, forces them to eat makeup and model themselves to death. Divine, playing one of the heavies, imagines himself to be Jackie during a dream sequence of the assassination. A still reproduced in the magazine shows Divine climbing out on the trunk of a car as a secret service agent (?) comes up the rear (the scene was apparently shot on the street where Waters' parents live in Baltimore).

'We didn't care who killed Kennedy,' says Waters. 'The point to us was how great Jackie looked through it.'

If this 1966 film really does exist, and it isn't a conceit of the Baltimore boy, two filmographies will have to be revised. *Mondo Trasho* (1969) is usually listed as Waters' first film, while Divine's first screen appearance is usually given as Waters' *Multiple Maniacs* (1970). *Eat Your Makeup* predates both.

[203] LEE OSWALD, ASSASSIN.
UK, 1966.
Director: Rudolph Cartier.
Made for TV. See No. 80.

[204] GREETINGS.

USA, 1968.
Directed by Brian De Palma.
Distributor: Eagle Production company: West End Films. Producer: Charles
Hirsch. Screenplay: Hirsch and De Palma. Photography: Robert Fiore. Editor:
De Palma. Music: The Children of Paradise.
CAST: Robert De Niro (Jon Rubin), Jonathan Warden (Paul Shaw), Gerrit Gra-
ham (Lloyd Clay), Megan McCormick (Marina).
    Richard Hamilton, the British pop artist, has a talking part but is
uncredited. He is the character talking about photographic blow-ups with Lloyd
in the park.
Eastman Color. Running time: 85/88 minutes.

Greetings is about three friends who receive their draft papers during the Vietnam war. Paul attempts to avoid military induction by making out he's gay
while Jon poses as a member of a top secret paranoid right-wing military group
with extremist views. Lloyd, however, is not going to let the draft stop him
from uncovering the truth about the JFK assassination. He develops a new
theory about the bullets' trajectories and meets a strange character in the
Bookmasters bookshop where he works who claims to be the seventeenth and
sole surviving witness to Lee Harvey Oswald's movements after the 'flight' from
the TSBD. The witness agrees to let Lloyd in on his research and gets him to
steal a copy of Josiah Thompson's *Six Seconds in Dallas*. Later, Lloyd is
himself assassinated at Battery Park while waiting for the witness who fails to
show up, presumably because he too has also been murdered. Lloyd thus
becomes the eighteenth witness to die. Jon ends up as the only one of the three
to be drafted. He goes to Vietnam and there continues his voyeuristic activities
by forcing a Vietnamese girl to undress for the TV cameras.
    There are passing references to the single bullet theory, the Warren *Report*,
Harold Weisberg and the critics and other related topics that show De Palma
has/had a more than nodding acquaintanceship with the assassination.
    The title comes from the opening line of the draft notice: 'Greetings from
the President of the United States.'
    Greetings was shot in two weeks on a $50,000 budget and reputedly went
into the black on the New York box office alone. It is a quirky and energetic
little film and has some imaginative moments, not least of which is Lloyd
marking Kennedy's wounds and plotting trajectories on his naked and half-
asleep girlfriend.
    A fine bit of film-making. Could it really have directed by the guy who gave
us *The Bonfire of the Vanities*? A sequel to *Greetings*, *Hi Mom!*, was made by
De Palma in 1968 and follows Jon, fresh back from Vietnam, in his new career
as a dirty movie producer.

For a note on De Palma's 1981 film, *Blow Out*, see the introductory matter at the beginning of this section.

See Michael Bliss' *Brian De Palma* (1983).

Guth and Wrone No. 2652.

[205] THE SERPENT.

USA, 1970.
NET film. See No. 95.

[206] EXECUTIVE ACTION.

USA, 1973.
Directed by David Miller.
Distributor: Scotia-Barber (UK). Production company: Executive Action Enterprises in association with Wakeford/Orloff Inc. Producer: Edward Lewis.
Screenplay: Dalton Trumbo. Story: Donald Freed and Mark Lane.
Photography: Robert Steadman. Editors: George Grenville and Irving Lerner.
Documentary editor: Ivan Dryer. Music: Randy Edelman.

Research: Robert Polin, Kevin Van Fleet, David Lifton, Lillian Castellano, Penn Jones, Jnr., Carol Rosenstein, Eda Hallinan, Barbara Elman.
CAST: Burt Lancaster (Farrington), Robert Ryan (Foster), Will Geer (Ferguson), Gilbert Green (Paulitz), John Anderson (Halliday), James MacColl (Lee Harvey Oswald/Oswald Impostor), Oscar Oncidi (Jack Ruby), etc.
Color. Running time: 91 minutes.

At the beginning of 1963 a group of right-wingers under the leadership of Foster (Robert Ryan) begin to formulate a plan to assassinate JFK who they see as a threat to their business and political interests. Two teams of marksmen are organised and trained by Farrington (Burt Lancaster, drawing on his experience in *Seven Days in May,* also produced by Edward Lewis). Dallas is decided upon for the 'execution' and through high level connections the plotters ensure the motorcade will pass in front of the TSBD where the chosen 'patsy,' Lee Harvey Oswald, works. Another conspirator in the group poses as the 'second Oswald' and lays further clues that will incriminate him. On 22 November JFK is killed in crossfire from gunmen on the Grassy Knoll, in the TSBD and in another building. After the assassination the gunmen escape with the help of other conspirators passing themselves off as Secret Service agents. Oswald is arrested and later shot by Jack Ruby who is on the periphery of the conspiracy.

The film was based upon the novel *Executive Action* (1973) written by Donald Freed and Mark Lane which, according to Guth and Wrone (pxxiv), was largely derived from James Hepburn's *Farewell America,* the typescript of which was delivered to Jim Garrison in New Orleans by Herve Lamarre, 'a person associated with French intelligence', while Lane himself was then down in the Crescent City helping out the District Attorney. The inference here clearly being that Lane ripped-off the French disinformation exercise.

The film credits Dalton Trumbo (one of the 'Hollywood Ten') with the screenplay and Freed and Lane with the story. Lane in his *Plausible Denial* (1991), p326, says that he had colloborated with Freed on the first draft of the screenplay but when they saw what happened to it in subsequent drafts (presumably by Trumbo) they protested both publicly and privately and their names were removed from the credits. Nevertheless, this doesn't stop Lane in the same book, opposite the main title page, giving himself sole credit for the screenplay.

All that remains in my memory from the two screenings I saw back in the mid-1970s are the fine performances from Burt Lancaster and Robert Ryan (it was his last film), the good use made of contemporary documentary footage and the ending that refers to the mysterious deaths of so many witnesses. The rest is a blank and much of this, I guess, is down to the pedestrian direction of David Miller (who only ever made one good film, *Lonely are the Brave* [1962]), not to mention Lane's glib 'solution.'

Available on video in the USA from Warner Home Video.

Guth and Wrone No. 2650.

[207] THE PARALLAX VIEW.

USA, 1974.
Director: Alan J. Pakula.
Distributor: CIC. Production company: Gus Productions in association with Harbor Productions and Doubleday Productions for Paramount. Executive producer: Gabriel Katzka. Producer: Alan J. Pakula. Executive producer: Gabriel Katzka. Producer: Alan J. Pakula. Screenplay: David Giler, Lorenzo Semple Jnr., based upon the novel by Loren Singer. Photography: Gordon Willis. Editor: John W. Wheeler. Music: Michael Small.
CAST: Warren Beatty (Joe Frady), Paula Prentiss (Lee Carter), William Daniels (Austin Tucker), Walter McGinn (Jack), Hume Cronyn (Rintels), Bill Joyce (Senator Carroll), etc.
Technicolor. Running time: 102 minutes.

Presidential aspirant Senator Carroll is assassinated at a political rally in Seattle. Journalist Lee Carter and her ex-lover, Joe Frady, witness this and the subsequent death of the 'lone' assassin.

Some years later Lee contacts Joe and tells him that witnesses to the assassination are being mysteriously killed and she feels she may be next. Frady becomes suspicious when Lee dies in an 'accident.' He visits a small mountain town where another witness has died and is nearly shot himself by the local sheriff. His research leads him to the sinister Parallax Corporation which is recruiting aggressive and disturbed misfits to be trained as assassins. Frady assumes another identity and enlists in the Parallax program. His identity is discovered by the Corporation and he is lured to a convention where Senator Hammond, a presidential contender, is assassinated by one of Parallax's hitmen. Frady attempts to escape and is shot by one of the trained assassins. A government report subsequently sticks the murder on Frady and says that he was a lone, mad assassin.

A film that was clearly inspired in part by the murder of JFK and the subsequent critical research. It's a fine bit of cinematic drama but, ultimately, the idea of the all-powerful all-knowing corporation belongs in the realms of hokum. As some critics have been heard to say, it's ideas like this that give conspiracy theories a bad name.

Guth and Wrone No. 2655.

[208] ANNIE HALL.

USA, 1977.
Directed by Woody Allen.
Script: Woody Allen and Marshall Brickman. Producer: Charles H. Joffe. Associate Producer: Fred T. Gallo. Executive Producer: Robert Greenhut. Photography: Gordon Willis. Editor: Ralph Rosenblum. A Jack Rollins - Charles H. Joffe Production. United Artists.
CAST: Woody Allen, Diane Keaton, Shelley Duvall, Tony Roberts, Christopher Walken, etc.
Color. Running time: 94 minutes.

This would be one of Allen's Top Five films were it not for the arch winsomeness of Diane Keaton.

There's an amusing scene near the beginning when Alvy Singer (Woody Allen) takes Allison Porchnik (Carol Kane) back to her apartment after an Adlai Stevenson rally. They are on the bed kissing and cuddling when Alvy suddenly stops, 'I'm sorry. I can't go through with this...it's obsessing me.' Allison says she is tired of his obsession with the JFK assassination, she needs his attention. Alvy wonders about the shots in Dealey Plaza and the conspiracy behind the assassination that probably involves everyone from Earl Warren to Lyndon Johnson, Hoover, the CIA and so on - everyone, in fact, except the men's room attendant at the White House. Allison accuses him: 'You're using this conspiracy theory as an excuse for not having sex with me!' Alvy turns to the camera in an aside: 'Oh, my God. She's right!'

[209] THE PRIVATE FILES OF J. EDGAR HOOVER.

USA, 1977.
Directed by Larry Cohen.
Distributor ITC (UK). Production company: Larco Productions. Producer: Larry Cohen. Screenplay: Larry Cohen. Photography: Paul Glickman. Editor: Christopher Lebenzon. Music: Miklos Rezsa.
CAST: Broderick Crawford (J. Edgar Hoover), Michael Parks (Robert F. Kennedy), Rip Torn (Dwight Webb Jnr.), Dan Dailey (Clyde Tolson), Raymond St. Jacques (Martin Luther King Jnr.), Andrew Duggan (Lyndon B. Johnson), Lloyd Gough (Walter Winchell), Jack Cassidy (Damon Runyon), William Jordan (John F. Kennedy), George D. Wallace (Senator Joseph McCarthy), Brooks Morton (Earl Warren), Richard Dixon (President Nixon), etc.
Color. Running time: 112 minutes.

This is the career of J. Edgar Hoover narrrated by an ex-FBI agent, Dwight Webb Jnr. It follows the Boss from his days as a young Justice Department lawyer through the rise of the Bureau to the years of corruption and chicanery (the 'private files'), and to his eventual death. With JFK in the White House and Bobby as Attorney General Hoover feels threatened and uses his knowledge of the Kennedy's Mafia connections as leverage for staying in place. Following JFK's death Hoover gets from Lyndon Johnson a waivering of his retirement in return for supplying the President with intelligence on his opponents. Following Hoover's death his aides secure the private files and begin shredding them so that they do not fall into the hands of the Nixon administration.

Larry Cohen's dense and complex film is one of the masterpieces of post-war Hollywood and a short notice like this can do no more than hint at its achievement. It's a film like *Citizen Kane* or *Once Upon a Time in America* - you need to see it a half-dozen times to appreciate it (though Broderick Crawford's rich portrayal of Hoover can be recognised from the first viewing).

Note: This should not be confused with *The Secret Files of J. Edgar Hoover*, a 1989 documentary first shown on US television and subsequently released on video that contains, *inter alia*, quite a bit of material on JFK and his involvement with Marilyn Monroe and Inga Arvad (and his alleged first marriage in 1939), but nothing on the assassination. Produced by Eric Leiber Productions and distributed by Western International Syndication. The UK video was released by Castle Communications in 1990.

[210] THE TRIAL OF LEE HARVEY OSWALD.

USA, 1977.
Director: David Greene.
Made for TV film. See No. 112.

[211] RUBY AND OSWALD [aka FOUR DAYS IN DALLAS].

USA, 1978.
Director: Mel Stuart.
Made for TV film. See No. 119.

[212] WINTER KILLS.

USA, 1979.
Directed by William Richert.
Distributor: ICA Projects (UK). Production company: Winter Gold Productions.
Executive producers: Leonard J. Goldberg and Robert Sterling. Screenplay:
William Richert, based upon the novel of the same title by Richard Condon.
Photography: Vilmos Zsigmond. Editor: David Bretherton. Music: Maurice
Jarre.
CAST: Jeff Bridges (Nick Kegan), John Huston (Pa Kegan), Anthony Perkins
(John Cerruti), Sterling Hayden (Z. K. Dawson), Eli Wallach (Joe Diamond),
Dorothy Malone (Emma Kegan), Ralph Meeker (Gameboy Baker), Toshiro Mi-
fune (Keith), Richard Boone (Keifetz), Elizabeth Taylor (Lola Camonte), etc.
Color. Running time: 96 minutes.

The story centers around Nick Kegan, the son of an immensely rich and
powerful businessman, Pa Kegan. Nick overhears a dying man's confession
that he was the 'second rifle' in the assassination of Nick's brother, a US
President. Through a complex and convoluted storyline Nick eventually traces
the plot back to his father and, possibly, John Cerruti, Pa Keegan's industrial
intelligence chief.
     Readers of Richard Condon's novel of the same name know that he used the
JFK assassination as a springboard for developing the story and the plot has
many points in common with actual events (the 'lone sniper' is subsequently
shot, and so on).
     Stanley Kubrick once said that bad books often make good films and vice
versa. This is the vice versa. What was credible and elegant in Richard
Condon's novel of the same name here becomes contrived and awkward. The
film, despite its pretensions, essentially projects a glossy *Dynasty*-style view of
America.

[213] BLOOD FEUD.

USA, 1980.
Director: Michael Newell.
Made for TV film. See No. 121.

[214] JACQUELINE BOUVIER KENNEDY.

USA, 1981.
Director: Stephen Gethers.
Made for TV film. See No. 125.

[215] KENNEDY.

UK, 1983.
Director: Jim Godard.
Made for TV film. See No. 128.

[216] FLASHPOINT.

USA, 1984.
Directed by William Tannen.
Distributor: Columbia-EMI-Warner (UK). Production company: Home Box Office in association with Silver Screen Partners. Producer: Skip Short. Co-producer: William Tannen. Screenplay by Dennis Shryack and Michael Butler, based upon the novel by George La Fountaine. Photography: Peter Moss. Editor: David Garfield. Music: Tangerine Dream.
CAST: Kris Kristofferson (Bob Logan), Treat Williams (Ernie Wiatt), Rip Torn (Sheriff Wells), Kevin Conway (Brook), Kurtwood Smith (Federal Inspector Carson), Roberts Blossom (Amarillo), etc.
Metrocolor. Running time: 94 minutes.

Bob Logan and Ernie Wiatt are Texas border patrolmen who have become disillusioned with their jobs. Logan chances upon a buried jeep in a dried-up river bed. Inside he finds the driver's skeleton, a high-powered rifle in a case, and $800,000 in pre-1963 bills. The two buddies see the cash as a means of escape. They stash the money at a deserted ranch and check the 1963 newspapers for details of the presumed robbery. The jeep is uncovered by a storm and is found by a desert recluse who is subsequently murdered, as are the two border patrolmen investigating the slaying. Meanwhile the area where the jeep was found is sealed off by a sinister Federal Inspector from Washington, Carson, and the military take over. Logan and Wiatt soon sense that Carson is behind the murders and after a series of chases in the desert Wiatt is killed. Logan is followed to the deserted ranch by Carson's men who attempt to kill him. Logan manages to kill them first and then make off with the money after being told by Sheriff Wells that the dead jeep driver was JFK's assassin.
This could so easily have been another bit of hokum but with fine performances by the two protagonists (particularly Kristofferson), Peter Moss' 'big screen' photography, and, notably, William Tannen's deft and understated

direction it becomes an enjoyable latterday western. Eight out of 10 for effort and imagination.

[217] CALL TO GLORY.

USA, 1985.
Director: Peter Levin.
Made for TV film. See No. 135.

[218] THE BIG EASY.

USA, 1986.
Directed by Jim McBride.
Producer: Stephen Friedman. Writer: Donald Petrie Jr. Editor: Mia Goldman.
Photography: Affonso Beato. Original music: Brad Fiedel.
CAST: Dennis Quaid, Ellen Barkin, Ned Beatty, Judge Jim Garrison, etc.
Color. Running time: 104 minutes.

Ellen Barkin plays an Assistant DA investigating police corruption in the New Orleans PD who falls in love with a detective played by Dennis Quaid. Early in the film Quaid is video-taped by the corruption task force receiving money from a bar owner and arrested. When his case comes to trial the court is presided over by Judge Jim Garrison playing himself.

[219] DOUBLE IMAGE [YURI NOSENKO, KGB].

UK, 1986.
Director: Mick Jackson.
Made for TV film. See No. 137.

[220] L.B.J.: THE EARLY YEARS.

USA, 1986.
Director: Peter Werner.
Made for TV film. See No. 140.

[221] TWILIGHT ZONE: Profile in Silver.

USA, 1986.
Episode in TV series. See No. 136.

[222] FULL METAL JACKET.

UK/USA, 1987.
Directed by Stanley Kubrick.
Produced by Stanley Kubrick. Screenplay by Stanley Kubrick, Michael Herr
and Gustav Hasford, based on Hasford's novel, *The Short-Timers.* Co-Producer:
Philip Hobbs. Executive Producer: Jan Harlan. Photography: Douglas Milsome.
Editor: Martin Hunter. Music: Abigail Mead. Warner Bros.
Color. Running time: 116 minutes.

The opening section of Kubrick's Vietnam movie is set in a Marine Corps boot-
camp in 1968 and is dominated by the non-stop obscene and violent dialogue
spat out by the Drill Instructor, Hartman, played with relish and conviction by
Lee Ermey, a one-time USMC sergeant himself.
   In Scene 34 (from the published screenplay, see in References under
Kubrick's name) the recruits are seated on bleachers out by the rifle range being
harangued by Hartman. He asks them if they know who Charles Whitman was?
Private Cowboy answers that he was the 'guy who shot all those people from
that tower in Austin, Texas.' Yes, says Hartman, he killed 20 people from
distances up to 400 yards. Now, the Drill Instructor continues, who was Lee
Harvey Oswald? He killed Kennedy, shouts a private, from that book
suppository (*sic*) building! Right, says Hartman, he scored two hits, including a
head shot, at a moving target from a distance of 250 feet. Whitman and Oswald
both learned to shoot in the Marine Corps, 'And before you ladies leave my
island, you will be able to do the same thing!'

[223] HOOVER VS. THE KENNEDYS [THE SECOND CIVIL WAR].

USA, 1987.
Director: Mike O'Herlihy.
Made for TV film. See No. 141.

[224] RUNNING AGAINST TIME.

USA, 1990.
Director: Bruce Seth Green.
Made for TV film. See No. 163.

[225] JFK.

USA, 1991.
Directed by Oliver Stone.
Distributors: Warner Bros. Production company: Le Studio Canal + Regency

Enterprises and Alcor Films - an Ixtlan Corporation and an A. Kitman Ho Production.

Producers: A Kitman Ho and Oliver Stone. Screenplay: Oliver Stone and Zachary Sklar based upon the books *On the Trail of the Assassins* by Jim Garrison (1988) and *Crossfire: The Plot That Killed Kennedy* by Jim Marrs (1989). Executive producer: Arnon Milchan. Photography: Robert Richardson. Editors: Joe Hutshing and Pietro Scalia. Music: John Williams

Technical advisors: Numa V. Bertel Jr., Bob Breall, Howard K. Davis, Dale Dye, Robert Groden, Roy Hargraves, Gerald P. Hemmings Jr., Larry Howard, Dr. Marion Jenkins, Ron Lewis, David Lifton, Jim Marrs, John Newman, Beverly Oliver, Col. L. Fletcher Prouty, Ellen Ray, Frank Ruiz, Gus Ruso, Perry Russo, Bob Spiegelman, John R. Stockwell, Cyril H. Wecht MD, JD, Stanley White, Tom Wilson.

Archival footage: Zapruder Film: "Copyright 1967" by LMH Company, All Rights Reserved. NBC News Archives. CBS News. UCLA Film and Television Archive. The Family of Orville O. Nix. Sherman Grindberg Film Libraries. Southern Methodist University thru its Southwest Film/Video Archives. National Archives. Cartoon clip courtesy of Warner Bros.

CAST: Kevin Costner (Jim Garrison), Sally Kirkland (Rose Cheramie), Zapruder (Ray LePere), Jay O. Sanders (Lou Ivon), Perry H. Russo (Angry Bar Patron), Ed Asner (Guy Bannister), Jack Lemon (Jack Martin), Gary Oldman (Lee Harvey Oswald), Sissy Spacek (Liz Garrison), Brian Doyle-Murray (Jack Ruby), Wayne Knight (Numa Bertel), Beata Pozniak (Marina Oswald), Tom Howard (Lyndon B. Johnson), Joe Pesci (David Ferrie), Walter Matthau (Senator Long), Pruitt Taylor Vince (Lee Bowers), Tony Plana (Carlos Bringuier), Tommy Lee Jones (Clay Shaw), John Candy (Dean Andrews), Kevin Bacon (Willie O'Keefe), Willem Oltmans (George de Mohrenschildt), Sally Nystuen (Mary Moorman), Jo Anderson (Julie Ann Mercer), etc. Technicolor. Running time: 189 minutes.

Hollywood has some good news and some bad news for the critics. The good news is that a major film is going to be made challenging the Warren *Report* and alleging a conspiracy. The bad news? Well, Jim Garrison is the hero.

This was pretty much the reaction throughout the critical community when news of Stone's film first began leaking out. How could Stone take Garrison seriously? Sure, we all thought, there is a film to be made out of what happened in New Orleans...but Big Jim as the hero?! Big Jim as the man who cracked the puzzle? It was hard to believe then and it's hard now after seeing the film. But here it is...Kevin Costner in 'Dances with Facts' aka *A Heritage of Stone* (the title of Garrison's 1970 book on the case), the film that argues Kennedy was killed because he was going to pull out of Vietnam.

As a moviegoer sitting in the middle stalls with a box of popcorn I thought it was a bravura piece of film-making, but as a critic I groaned, and still groan.

But it's the best we've got and it has introduced the assassination to a couple of generations who knew little or nothing about it, and it's got them thinking. When I saw the picture at a local multi-screen cinema it was the third week and there wasn't an empty seat. I was the only one in the audience old enough to have been around when it happened. Everybody else was under 30 years of age.

There are some striking performances in the film, notably by Tommy Lee Jones as Clay Shaw, Ed Asner as Guy Bannister, John Candy as Dean Andrews, and Donald Sutherland as 'X' (Fletcher Prouty) which throw into relief Kevin Costner's strangely languid portrayal of the film's hero. Gary Oldman's Oswald despite all the ballyhoo was a mere cipher (which may have been what Stone wanted). Garrison himself appears as Earl Warren (a nice irony) while the Jolly Green Giant's star witness Perry Russo has a cameo as an Angry Bar Patron.

Stone makes good use of contemporary photographs and footage and includes both the Nix and Zapruder films in their entirety (seeing Zapruder on the big screen for the first time makes one realise how much detail is lost on a TV screen).

Stone went to Dallas and transformed Dealey Plaza to make it appear as it did in 1963 - trees were lopped, the exterior of the TSBD was returned to its original appearance and the sixth floor was re-created as it was at the time of the assassination. Stone also shot at the Texas Theater, Oswald's boarding house, the Dallas PD and in the neighbourhood where Tippit was shot. In New Orleans he filmed in the Criminal Courts Building where the Shaw trial took place. 10 out of 10 for locations.

The screenplay was written by Stone and Zachary Sklar and based upon Garrison's *On the Trail of the Assassins* (1988) and Jim Marrs' *Crossfire* (1989). Sklar, a former executive editor of *The Nation* magazine, had edited Garrison's book for the publishers, Sheridan Square Press. He has also edited Ralph McGehee's *Deadly Deceits: My 25 Years in the CIA* and Melvin Beck's *Secret Contenders: The Myth of Cold War Counter-Intelligence*.

As I have noted above the Garrison case does present good dramatic possibilities for a film-maker intent on representing what actually happened as opposed to mythologising the New Orleans DA. Similarly, we still need a good critical revionist investigation into the case. Henry Hurt went some way to realising this in a chapter in *Reasonable Doubt* (1985). The best and most detailed book on the actual trial remains the one written from the Shaw camp, James Kirkwood's *American Grotesque* (1970). James DiEugenio's *Destiny Betrayed* (1992) is essential and future commentators on the Garrison case will ignore it at their peril.

Further references: Oliver Stone's apologia and defense, 'November 22, 1963: Oliver Stone Talks Back' appeared in the January 1992 issue of *Esquire*. This can be profitably bracketed with the 15 page interview with Stone dated 25 November 1991 that was included in the JFK press-kit put out by Warner Bros.

Norman Mailer's fannish review, 'Footfalls in the Crypt,' graced the pages of the February 1992 *Vanity Fair*. Anthony Summers' 'Who Killed JFK: The Unstoned Version' while uncharacteristically shrill is well argued and provocative and was on the front of the 'Weekend' section of *The Independent* (London), 15 February 1992. Clifford Krauss' '28 Years After Kennedy's Assassination, Conspiracy Theories Refuse to Die' in the *New York Times*, 5 January 1992, is worth a peek if for no other reason than the quote it ends with - Robert Blakey at his best: 'There isn't a single witness left to bring in. The people out there are all people with theories.' This precisely echoes the new establishment revisionism: Earl Warren may not have done a good job but now it's too late to do anything about it (so let's all go home).

The best account of the background to the film and the media response to its making is Robert Sam Anson's 'The Man Who Shot JFK' in the February 1992 *Esquire*. Anson revealed that it was Harold Weisberg who gave a copy of the JFK script to George Lardner for his rubbishing essay in the *Washington Post*. Stone called Lardner 'a CIA agent-journalist,' and Mark Lane has said of him 'that he has never seen a CIA report he hasn't fallen in love with.' Lardner, it may be recalled, was the last known person to see David Ferrie alive.

A review-essay of the film is Chapter 26 of Harrison Livingstone's *High Treason 2* (1992), pps521-45, which has many good points to make but is marred by its tendentiousness. Carl Oglesby's thoughts on the film and its reception by the media are in Part V of his *The JFK Assassination* (1992), pps261-302. Oglesby is a fine stylist and can clarify and get to the heart of an argument in a trice. 'JFK: The Second Coming of Jim Garrison' by Edward J. Epstein is included in Epstein's *The Assassination Chronicles* (1992), pps571-81.

Applause Books in New York have published the illustrated *JFK: The Book of the Film* (1992). This includes the full screenplay with a research gloss and nearly 100 critical pieces, pro and con, arising from the movie amongst which are Robert Sam Anson's and Norman Mailer's pieces noted above. Curiously, three writers withheld permission for articles they had written to be included - George Will, Arlen Specter, Anthony Summers. Responses by Oliver Stone and interviews with him are also included. The 593-page book includes the film's full credits. An essential work.

JFK was released on video in the US by Warner Home Video in 1992 and in the UK in September 1992. In the US it has also been issued on laser disc.

[226] RUBY.

USA, 1992.
Directed by John Mackenzie.
A Triumph Releasing Corporation release of a Polygram presentation of a Propaganda Films presentation. Producers: Sigurjon Sighvatsson, Steve Golin.

Executive Producer: Michael Kuhn. CoProducer: Jay Roewe. Associate Producers: Richard Wright, Lynn Weimer. Screenplay: Stephen Davis, based upon his play *Love Field*. Camera: Phil Meheux. Editor: Richard Trevor. Music: John Scott. Production Design: David Brisbin. Art Director: Kenneth A. Hardy. Costume Design: Susie DeSanto. Sound: David Brownlow.

Special optical enhancement of motorcade footage by Robert Groden. Stock footage: Robert Groden, J. Fred MacDonald and Associates, John F. Kennedy Library Foundation, CBS News Archives, NBC News Archives, Worldwide Television News.

CAST: Danny Aiello (Jack Ruby), Sherilynn Fenn (Candy Cane), Arliss Howard (Maxwell), Tobin Bell (David Ferrie), David Duchovny (Officer Tippit), Richard Sarafian (Proby), Marc Lawrence (Santos Alicante), Willie Garson (Lee Harvey Oswald), Joe Viterelli (Joseph Valachi), Carmine Caridi (Sam Giancana), Gerard David (John F. Kennedy), May Chris Wall (Jackie Kennedy), etc.

Deluxe Color. Running time: 106 minutes.

This is a preposterous fictionalized biography of Jack Ruby following him through the year that ends soon after JFK's assassination. The film shows Mob and CIA involvement in the assassination but in such a way that one can only conclude the writer, Stephen Davis, knows little or nothing about the background to the events of 22 November. Here we have Ruby picking up a waif at the bus station who turns out to be a stripper, Candy Cane (echoes of Candy Barr?), giving her a break at the Carousel Club and then flying with her to a Mobsters' convention in Las Vegas where she meets and goes to bed with JFK. David Ferrie is at the convention too (and with his own hair yet), mooching about like a game-show host on Valium. Enter Maxwell, the CIA operative, who gives the JFK contract to...Ruby, no less. Good old Jack balks at the assignment and it is left to others to execute the hit. Ruby then shoots Oswald because he was one of the plotters.

The film's production values are cheap, the direction pedestrian, and even the lighting is flat. In the words of the *Variety* review, 30 March 1992, *Ruby* has 'homevideo written all over it and doesn't figure to shine too brightly at the box office'. A poor film from John Mackenzie, a British director who knows better. He made *The Long Good Friday,* probably the best British gangster film after Mike Hodges' *Get Carter*.

The film is based on a play, *Love Field,* by the British writer, Stephen Davis, that was first performed at the Bush Theatre in London during the mid-1980s. Davis also wrote *Double Image*, the BBC dramatization of Yuri Nosenko's defection, No. 137 above.

9

Lost, Unconfirmed, Spurious, Unrealized, and Forthcoming Films

In alphabetical order under title.

[227] ALEXANDER, STEVEN L.
A professional cameraman who covered Dallas from the evening of the assassination through to the shooting of Oswald. Whereabouts of footage unknown.
See Weisberg's *Photographic Whitewash* (1976), p121.

[228] AUTOPSY FILM - JFK.
Dennis David has claimed that Lieutenant-Commander William Bruce Pitzer filmed the JFK autopsy at Bethesda Naval Hospital. While there is no reason to doubt David's word the film has never surfaced, but then neither has much of the other material arising from the autopsy at the Bethesda morgue on the night of the 22/23 November 1963.
Pitzer was found dead at the Naval Hospital on 29 October 1966. He had a gunshot wound on the right side of the head. The authorities ruled that it was a suicide, yet Pitzer was lefthanded. This was the same day the Kennedy family transferred the autopsy materials from Bethesda to the National Archives, which may or may not be significant.
See Harrison Livingstone's *High Treason 2* (1992), pps556-9, for an examination of the alleged suicide.

[229] MRS. BECK(?).
On 5 December 1963 an unidentified woman contacted the Detroit office of the FBI and said she had 16mm color footage of the assassination that was better than the photographs recently published in *Life* magazine. She said she would post the film to the office.
On the same day Robert Lubeck, Features Editor of the *Detroit News*, re-

ceived a phone call from a Mrs. Beck of Lincoln Park, Michigan, who would not identify herself further, saying that she had 16mm color film of the assassination taken from the overpass. She too said the film was better than *Life*'s pictures.

The two women would appear to be one and the same.

The undated FBI memo (probably mid-December 1964) reporting the two calls and detailing the subsequent 'dead end' investigations is reproduced in Weisberg's *Photographic Whitewash* (1976), p288.

I have never been able to put my finger on why this FBI memo seems so fishy, perhaps it is because all the leads end so patly (according to the FBI). Some futher investigation is called for here.

[230] CBS-TV OUTTAKES.
In the spring of 1966 Emile de Antonio and Mark Lane viewed some five hours of an estimated 70 hours of outtakes from the four-part CBS documentary on the JFK assassination, No. 84 above.

Originally de Antonio and Lane were granted permission to use this footage but the decision was later reversed. The remainder of the footage was never seen. As Lane points out, what they saw were the 'working documents' that told a different story from the carefully-edited broadcast version.

Is all this footage still in existence?

See Mark Lane's *A Citizen's Dissent* (1968), p188 *et seq.*

[231] CROSSFIRE VIDEO.
Jim Marrs, author of *Crossfire* (1989), intends to produce a companion video according to the January 1987 issue of *The Third Decade*. Marrs has, however, been involved with three other videos, Nos. 162, 168 and 171.

[232] DALLAS BELLES [aka MODERN MOTEL].
This is a 10 minute b&w porno loop allegedly shot in a Dallas motel in the mid-1950s and featuring several of Ruby's girls. One shot shows Jack Ruby himself buggering a girl dressed in cow-girl costume.

The film was mentioned to me by an assassination buff while I was living in Los Angeles in the late 1960s. The buff lived just off Santa Monica Blvd., out near the beach. I cannot even remember his full name now. It was Harry followed by an Armenian-sounding surname like but not Arounian. Whenever I asked to see the pic he would say that it was out on loan or that he could not find it. Harry claimed the film was shot in a motel in Dallas and was also known under the title of *Modern Motel*. He reckoned that Ruby was easily recognisable despite his efforts to keep his face away from the camera and that the girls were all 'obvious show-girl types'.

I am not doubtful as to the film's existence but I am doubtful to the identity of Ruby and his show-girls. Curiously though, one of the most famous and popular porno films of all time *was* shot in a Dallas motel in the 1950s and did feature a professional stripper who did dress up in cow-girl costume. This is *Smart Aleck* that was made in 1951 and featured a young Candy Barr (real name Juanita Slusher). Did Jack Ruby have anything to do with this film? The Mob have always been involved in pornography and is it not reasonable to suppose that their man in Dallas would have maintained this interest? Nancy Hamilton while being interviewed by Mark Lane for *Rush to Judgement,* No. 85, claimed that Ruby ran girls, and from running them to filming them is but a small step.

A soft-core exploitation film featuring one of Ruby's girls has been going the rounds lately. This is *Mondo Exotic,* originally made in 1963 and featuring the stripper Jada (Janet Adams Conforto). Did Ruby have a hand in making this? A clip is included in *The Men Who Killed Kennedy,* No. 142.

The fullest stag filmography is in Di Lauro and Rabkin's *Dirty Movies* (1976), pps125-58, and runs to over 30 pages of double columns. They do not list *Dallas Belles* or *Modern Motel,* but there are entries for two versions of *Motel Moderne,* both made sometime between 1951 and 1954, and both featuring a single man and woman only.

See further note on *Dallas Belles* in the Addenda below.

[233] DAVID FERRIE IN DEALEY PLAZA?
Joachim Joesten in *The Garrison Enquiry: Truth and Consequences* (1967) mentions that an individual who was in Ferrie's Civil Air Patrol saw television coverage from Dealey Plaza at the time of the assassination in which he recognised Ferrie.

[234] THE DAY THEY BLEW KENNEDY'S HEAD OFF AND LEFT JUST A
    BLOODY STUMP.
An invented title for a non-existent film featured in Brian McCormick's wickedly funny 'Journal of the Making of an Antinuclear Feminist Clayworks Statement on Mental Retardation' in *National Lampoon,* October 1981.

[235] THE LAST TWO DAYS.
A video noted in *The Third Decade,* September 1985, p18, note 1, as comprising *President Kennedy's Last Hour,* No. 35, together with a 'little-known film shot by a member of the White House staff who was three cars behind the President in the Dallas motorcade' (No. 46). No date given.

[236] LIBRA.
This is the proposed film of Don DeLillo's ponderous and unconvincing novelization of Lee Harvey Oswald's life that was published in 1988.

Time, 10 June 1991, reported that 'According to Hollywood sources, the director [Oliver Stone] has worked hard to block a movie based on...*Libra*'. The magazine then quoted Dale Pollack, president of A&M Films, who had acquired the film rights of the DeLillo book, that 'Stone has a right to make his film, but he doesn't have a right to try and stop everyone else from making their films.' Stone may be big in Tinseltown but I doubt he has the power to stop anyone else from making a film. The protest sounds too much like a let-off, and anyway he, Stone, did not prevent John Mackenzie's *Ruby* being released hot on the heels of *JFK* (or being filmed in Dallas at the same time).

[237] DAVID LIFTON VIDEO.
Lifton has been working on a follow-up to the *Best Evidence* video, No. 165, for sometime.

[238] HARRISON LIVINGSTONE VIDEO.
Harrison Livingstone, co-author with Robert Groden of *High Treason* (1989), and sole author of *High Treason 2* (1992), gathered together in April 1991 at the Stouffer Hotel in Dallas several of the Bethesda autopsy personnel and some of the doctors and nurses from Parkland for the first time. The proceedings were filmed by the Fisher Production Group.

A still from the film is reproduced opposite p225 of *High Treason 2* showing: Floyd Riebe, Paul O'Connor, James Curtis Jenkins, Harrison Livingstone, Aubrey Rike, Dr. Robert McClelland, Nurse Audrey Bell, and Dr. Philip Williams.

Livingstone has not responded to several letters requesting further details.

[239] GEORGE DE MOHRENSCHILDT - NOS-TV (Netherlands).
Willem Oltmans, a Dutch journalist, originallly interviewed George and Jeanne de Mohrenschildt in 1964. He cultivated the friendship and in 1969 taped a long interview with the couple. George said that he did not believe Oswald acted alone and he named a number of figures involved, he said, in a much wider conspiracy.

In 1976 Oltmans approached de Mohrenschildt with the backing of a major Dutch TV company - NOS. He wanted George to tell him everything he knew, and tell it on camera. An undisclosed amount of film was shot and de Mohrenschildt even travelled to Amsterdam for further filmed interviews in March 1977. Two weeks after arriving back in the States George was dead from an alleged self-inflicted gunshot wound.

NOS presumably still has the filmed interviews but I have found no record of them being shown.

There is a good account of the bizarre Oltmans/de Mohrenschildt episodes in Dick Russell's *The Man Who Knew Too Much* (1992), pps279-83. See also on Oltmans the article by Scott Van Wynsberghe, 'Some Notes on Occult Irrationalism and the Kennedy Assassination,' in *Lobster* (Hull), December 1992.

[240] ROBERT MORROW: FIRST HAND KNOWLEDGE.

A flyer from Shapolsky Publishers, Inc., of New York announces the forthcoming September 1992 publication of Robert Morrow's *First Hand Knowledge: How I Participated in the CIA-Mafia Murder of President Kennedy*. The revelations include the CIA's assassination plan, the involvment of Richard Nixon and LBJ, the role of Carlos Marcello, and the prior knowledge of Allen Dulles. This book, the flyer continues, 'is the basis of a major PBS *Frontline* TV-special (September 1992)'.

If my memory serves me right this is about the third book on the assassination written by Morrow. I have never been able to get past the first page of either of his previous books and, further, I have never met anyone who has taken his claims seriously. Could we all be wrong?

[241] BEVERLY OLIVER: THE 'BABUSHKA LADY.'

Beverly Oliver was 19 at the time of the assassination, working at the Colony Club in Dallas, a strip joint next door to Ruby's Carousel Club. She took a Yashica Super-8mm movie camera to Dealey Plaza to film the President and positioned herself on the grassy triangle south of Elm. She was standing behind Charles Brehm and opposite Abraham Zapruder, and she is clearly seen in many photographs taken on the day. She began filming approximately 15 seconds before the first shot was fired and continued to about 10 seconds after the last shot.

Thus Oliver filmed the entire assassination as the motorcade moved along Elm. She would also have captured the TSBD as the shots were fired and the 'umbrella man' and his dark colleague on the north of Elm, not to mention the Grassy Knoll at the time of the head shot.

On the Monday after the assassination two men came up to her near the Colony Club and told her that they knew she had shot film in Dealey Plaza. Oliver believed the men were either from the FBI or Secret Service. It is thought that Regis Kennedy, an FBI officer, was one of them (Kennedy was an agent in the FBI's New Orleans office while Oswald was in the Crescent City, and later refused to answer Jim Garrison's questions about a Clay Shaw investigation immediately after the assassination). They explained to her that they needed the film for evidence and that if she would give it to them they would return it within 10 days. She handed the film over and never saw it again. There it seems to disappear from history.

The Dallas *Times Herald* in November 1978 wrote of the HSCA's discovery of the Charles Bronson film and continued, 'A high official of the Select Committee says he remembers only two incidents in the two-year investigation of the slaying of such apparently new film coming to life. One concerned a Dallas woman who supposedly turned some film over to the FBI, but which was supposedly lost by the Bureau. This footage was later found, he said.'

In May 1979 Gary Shaw asked Robert Blakey about the newspaper report and he denied any knowledge of the Oliver film. A little over a week later, however, Blakey was interviewed by Earl Goltz of the *Dallas Morning News* who described what the film is believed to show. Blakey counteracted with a curious response: 'Oh, yeah, I am pretty certain we had it...if so, it didn't show much.' Whether this response was merely bravado on Blakey's part in an attempt to forestall any further questioning of his report or not we do not know. It is relevant to note that three other people believe that HSCA did have Oliver's film - Robert Groden, FBI agent James Hosty, and 'a very reliable source' who spoke to Christopher Scally in October 1979 saying that Blakey had organised a secret showing of the film for certain members of the Committee's staff (see Scally's *'So Near... and Yet So Far'* [nd], pps81-3).

Oliver knew Jack Ruby and Ruby once introduced her to 'Lee Oswald of the CIA.' She also claims David Ferrie was a frequent visitor to Ruby's club.

For an intriguing account of Oliver see Jim Marrs' *Crossfire* (1989), pps36-7. An extended video interview of Oliver by Mark Oakes is noted at No. 175.

[242] PLAUSIBLE DENIAL.

Opposite the main title page of Mark Lane's *Plausible Denial* (1991) he lists the screenplay of the book amongst his credits. At the time of going to press I have not been able to obtain further details.

Plausible Denial is an account of Lane defending the Liberty Lobby (successfully, it may be added) in a suit of defamation brought by E. Howard Hunt. The action arose from an article published by the Liberty Lobby and written by Victor Marchetti that alleged Hunt, the ex-CIA operative and convicted Watergate burglar, was involved in the JFK assassination.

[243] A PRESIDENT ON THE CROSSHAIRS.

According to Victor Ostrovsky in his book, *By Way of Deception* (1990), pps141-3, this was the title of a Mossad training film that he saw sometime in the 1980s. It is a detailed study of the JFK assassination made by the Israeli intelligence agency for training purposes.

Mossad believed the target of the assassination was not Kennedy but John Connally - targeted by Mafia hit men who were trying to muscle in on the Texas oil business. The agency simulated the Dealey Plaza scene and proved that Oswald could not have achieved what was claimed for him. Oswald was a dupe. 'The Mossad had every film taken of the Dallas assassination, pictures of the area, the topography, aerial photographs, everything. Using mannequins they duplicated the presidential cavalcade over and over again.'

Ostrovsky worked for Mossad for four years, but until some independent corroboration for the film's existence comes along, I think we can safely dismiss it.

See Scott Van Wynsberghe's 'Stray Shots VII: What the Mossad Knows' in

The Third Decade, September 1991.

[244] SWEDISH (TELEVISION?) DOCUMENTARY.
There is a tantalizing reference to this in Mark Lane's *A Citizen's Dissent*
(1968), p90, where he writes that a 'filmed documentary' was produced in
Sweden 'by a leading historian and professor of historical records at the
University of Stockholm'. A superior footnote figure after the word Stockholm
leads back to the 'Citations' at the end of the book where the following appears:
'Docent Hans Villius, University of Stockholm' (not Notes or References, but
Citations. Only Lane would use such a term in this context).

[245] THE THREE TRAMPS.
In the samizdat *JFK Assassination Solved!* underground paper (no date):
'Tramps Hunt and Sturgis and "Doe," actual arrest, live, behind Grassy Knoll
for JFK's murder. Original Super-8 sound live! $20.'
   The Three Tramps or the Three Stooges?

[246] UNDERGROUND MOVIES?
I have heard of several 1960s underground movies with titles alluding to the
Kennedy assassination, but these ephemeral political statements mostly seem to
have gone the way of old nitrate stock. An obsessive researcher might trawl
1960s runs of *Film Culture* and *The Village Voice* for leads and details.
   See *The Day They Blew...*, No. 234, for an archetypal underground title (if
invented).

[247] UNIVERSAL PICTURES NEWSREEL.
In the London-published *Today* magazine, 15 February 1964, there appeared an
article entitled 'Did Two Gunmen Cut Down Kennedy?' written by Larry Ross,
an associate of Mark Lane's though not mentioned in Lane's *A Citizen's Dissent*
(1968).
   Ross writes: 'But even estimates [of the time frame of the shots] of four or
five seconds may be too high. Stopwatch timing of the shots heard on the Universal Pictures newsreel indicate that only 3.1 seconds elapsed from first to
third shot.'
   3.1 seconds? Stopwatch timing of the Universal Pictures newsreel? Is this an
invention, a misunderstanding, or what?
   I can find no trace of a Universal Pictures newreel. Ross must mean
Universal Newsreel that ran from December 1951 to October 1967 in the US.
The programs are archived at Halcyon Days Productions and Film/Audio
Services, both in New York, Nos. 254 and 255 respectively, below.

[248] UNKNOWN NEWSREEL.
Here may be included all of the newsreels and documentary footage that have

mysteriously disappeared. Here could be the film that really does answer the question: Who killed Kennedy?

[249] ROSCOE WHITE FILM.
Apart from everything else, it is claimed that White left behind a can of film.

A 10x8 of Mark Lane suitable for framing will be given to the reader with the most plausible suggestion as to what it contains.

[250] WORLD IN ACTION.
World in Action is the award-winning British television investigative program that has been running for over 25 years. According to Duncan Crow in his book, *World in Action* (1965), a team from the program led by Tim Hewat flew out to Dallas immediately after the assassination and a report was broadcast in the UK on 28 November 1963 (Thanksgiving Day in the USA).

Crow, ps45-50, prints what appears to be an edited transcript of the program. This shows that Hewat seemed to concentrate more on the city of Dallas and its reactions to the assassination than any investigation into the event itself. Tom Howard, Ruby's defense counsel was interviewed, as was the town mayor, Earle Cabell.

10

North American Film, TV, and Newsreel Libraries with Assassination Footage

Here are listed the main libraries with assassination footage. There may well be important material housed in smaller and lesser known collections. The dedicated researcher intent on undertaking such a vast search should begin with *Footage 89: North American Film and Video Sources* and its supplement, *Footage 91* (New York: Prelinger Associates, 1989, 1991) which list over 1600 film and video collections.

[251] ABC NEWS.

ABC News: 47 West 66th Street, New York, NY 10023. Telephone: 212-456-7777.
News programing from 1963 to date. Some material is also available from Sherman Grinberg, No. 263.

[252] CANADIAN BROADCASTING CORPORATION (CBC).

CBC - Stock Shot Research and Sales: P.O. Box 500, Terminal A, Toronto, ON M5W 1E6, Canada. Telephone: 416-975-7608.

[253] CBS NEWS ARCHIVES.

CBS News Archives: 524 West 57th Street, New York, NY 10019. Telephone: 212-975-2875/2876.

[254] FILM/AUDIO SERVICES.

Film/Audio Services Inc.: 430 West 14th Street, Room 402, New York, NY 10014. Telephone: 212-645-2112.
Includes US government films and Universal Newsreel cut stories and outtakes.

[255] HALCYON DAYS PRODUCTIONS.

Halcyon Days Productions: 12 West End Avenue, 5th Floor, New York, NY 10023. Telephone: 212.397.8785.
Holds the Universal Newreel Library and some JFK home movies.

[256] JOHN F. KENNEDY LIBRARY.

The John F. Kennedy Library: Columbia Point, Boston, MA 02125. Telephone: 617.929.4538.
The largest single collection of film and TV material relating to President Kennedy, but little on the assassination and the ensuing controversy.

[257] LIBRARY OF CONGRESS.

Library of Congress - Motion Picture, Broadcasting and Recorded Sound Division: Room 336, Madison Building, Washington, DC 20540. Telephone: 202.707.1000.
Includes vast TV and newsreel collections. The Library of Congress is not, however, primarily a licensing body.

[258] MACDONALD AND ASSOCIATES.

J. Fred MacDonald and Associates: 2744 West Rascher Avenue, Chicago, IL 60625. Telephone: 312.878.4799.
Large newsreel and TV library with a JFK Assassination Archive that includes news outtakes from Kennedy's Texas trip.

[259] THE MUSEUM OF TELEVISION AND RADIO.

The Museum of Television and Radio: 25 West 52nd Street, New York, NY 10019. Telephone: 212.621.6600.
In addition to the comprehensive collection of television broadcasts the Museum contains much radio news material.

[260] NATIONAL ARCHIVES AND RECORDS ADMINISTRATION
(NARA).

NARA, Motion Picture, Sound and Video Branch: 7th and Pennsylvania
Avenue NW, Room 2W, Washington DC 20408. Telephone:
202-501-5449/5626.
As well as a vast collection of films made by or for the US Government the ar-
chives also house Universal Newsreel releases and outtakes, Fox Movietone
News, News of the Day and other commercially produced newsreels.

[261] NBC NEWS.

NBC News Video Archives: 30 Rockefeller Plaza, Room 922, New York, NY
10112. Telephone: 212-664-3797.
All of the broadcast material and some outtakes.

[262] PUBLIC BROADCASTING SYSTEM (PBS).

PBS - Program Data and Analysis; 1320 Braddock Place, Alexandria, VA
22314-1698. Telephone: 703.739.5000.
Includes all of the House Select Committee on Assassinations hearings
broadcast by PBS in 1978 (see No. 117).

[263] SHERMAN GRINBERG.

Sherman Grinberg Film Libraries Inc.: 630 Ninth Avenue, New York, NY
10036-3787. Telephone 212-765-5170. 1040 North McCadden Place, Hollywood, CA 90038-2486. Telephone: 213-464-7491.
Footage from ABC News and other contemporary sources including Pathe
news. Extensive holdings of JFK assassination related material.

[264] SOUTHERN METHODIST UNIVERISTY.

Southern Methodist University - Southwest Film/Video Archives: PO
Box 4194, Dallas, TX 75275. Telephone: 214.373.3665.
Aside from the Gene Autry Film Collection and the Ginger Rogers Film
Collection SMU also houses the Belo Newsfilm Collection containing all the
news footage from WFAA-TV in Dallas from 1960-75 (including outtakes).

[265] TWENTIETH CENTURY FOX - MOVIETONEWS.

Twentieth Century Fox - Movietonews Inc.: 460 West 54th Street, New York,
NY 10019. Telephone: 212-556-2560.

Contains the Movietonews releases and outtakes.

[266] UNIVERSITY OF CALIFORNIA - LOS ANGELES (UCLA).

UCLA Film and Television Archive: 1438 Melnitz Hall, UCLA, Los Angeles, CA 90024. Telephone: 213-206-8013.
Telenews, Hearst Metrotone News and other newsreels.

[267] UNIVERSITY OF SOUTH CAROLINA.

USC Newsfilm Library: Instructional Services Center, Columbia, SC 29208. Telephone: 803-777-6841.
Movietonews newsreels and also local NBC TV news.

[268] VANDERBILT UNIVERSITY.

Vanderbilt University - Television News Archive: Jean and Alexander Heard Library, 419 21st Avenue South, Nashville, TN 37240-0007. Telephone: 615-322-2927.
The largest collection of television newscasts in the US.

[269] VISNEWS.

Visnews International: 630 Fifth Avenue, 7th Floor, New York, NY10111. Telephone: 212-698-4513.
One of the largest newsreel and stock footage libraries in the world, jointly owned by NBC, Reuters and the BBC. The Library is actually located in London but can be researched from New York (see No. 273).

[270] WORLDWIDE TELEVISION NEWS (WTN).

WTN: 1995 Broadway, 11th Floor, New York, NY 10023. Telephone: 212-362-4440.
Footage includes UPI News and UPI-Worldwide Television News.

11

United Kingdom Film, TV, and Newsreel Libraries with Assassination Footage

[271] BRITISH MOVIETONE NEWS.

British Movietone News Ltd: North Orbital Road, Denham, Uxbridge, Middlesex UB9 5HQ, England. Telephone (01144) 895.833071.
The library holds *The Last Journey,* an 800ft newsreel compilation screened in November 1963 showing post-assassination scenes in Dealey Plaza, Oswald in custody, Ruby slaying Oswald, and concentrating chiefly on the funeral in Washington. The Dallas material is virtually the same as the Pathe newreel (see below).

[272] BRITISH PATHE NEWS.

British Pathe News Ltd: Pinewood Studios, Pinewood Road, Iver Heath, Buckinghamshire SL0 ONH, England. Telephone (01144) 753.630361.
Archived is the newsreel described at No. 68 (probably sourced from the Sherman Grinberg library in New York).

[273] VISNEWS.

Visnews Ltd: Cumberland Avenue, London NW10 7EH, England. Telephone: (01144) 819.657733.
One of the largest newsreel libraries in the world. See also No. 269 above.

12

Addenda

[274] FATAL FRIDAY.
A film documentary produced by Gordon McLendon, the pioneer Texas radio broadcaster. Copy held in McLendon Archive at the Texas Tech University - Southwest Collection, PO Box 4090, Lubbock, TX 79409.

    McLendon operated the Dallas radio station KLIF and used it for promoting extreme conservative views. Weird Beard, a KLIF disc-jockey, has stated that Jack Ruby greatly admired McLendon and, indeed, Ruby is alleged to have telephoned McLendon on the night of 22 November 1963. McLendon was a former Navy Intelligence officer who knew J. Edgar Hoover. He died of cancer, aged 65, on 14 September 1987.

[275] GARY SHAW AND THE KENNEDY ASSASSINATION.
An episode in the *Alternative Views* public affairs cable program broadcast by Austin (Texas) Community Television (ACTV). Copy with Alternative Information Network, PO Box 7279, Austin, TX 78712.

[276] HE MUST HAVE SOMETHING.
A documentary produced by Stephen Tyler examing the Garrison investigation and broadcast by WLAE-TV in New Orleans on 9 February 1992. Judge Haggerty who presided over the Clay Shaw trial is interviewed and says that 'Shaw lied through his teeth' and did 'a con job on the jury.'

[277] THE PLOT TO KILL KENNEDY.
Released in the US by Sun Classic Pictures/Taft International in 1980.

[278] UNCLASSIFIED: THE PLOT TO KILL PRESIDENT KENNEDY.
This was the title given to the 1983 video, *The Plot to Kill President Kennedy:*

From the De-Classified Files, No. 134, when it was reissued in a revised version in 1989.

[279] 11-22-63: THE DAY A NATION CRIED.
A PBS-TV documentary about the Kennedy presidency that touches on the assassination incidentally. Live coverage from Dallas station WFAA-TV is used and various interviews. Endorses the Warren *Report* findings.
Narrated by James Earl Jones and first broadcast in 1988.

[280] NBC NEWS: Malcolm Kilduff.
Gary Mack reports in *Cover-Ups!,* May 1985, that found in the NBC film archives is a 22 November 1963 interview with White House press aide Malcolm Kilduff who quotes the President's personal physician, Admiral George Burkley, as saying Kennedy was shot in the right temple.

[281] A WOMAN NAMED JACKIE.
Thames Television, London. 6 and 7 September 1992. Director: Larry Peerce. Color. Running time: 250 minutes.
Executive Producer: Lester Persky. Producer: Lorin Bennett Salob. Co-Producer: Tomlinson Dean. Teleplay: Roger O. Hirson, based upon C. David Heymann's biography, *A Woman Named Jackie* (New York, 1989). Photography: Mike Fash. Production Designer: Stewart Campbell. Film Editor: Susan B. Browdy. Music: Lalo Schifrin. Archival Film: John F. Kennedy Library, NBC News Archives. Lester Persky Productions in association with World International Network. Copyright 1991 Lester Persky Productions Inc.
CAST: Roma Downey (Jackie Kennedy/Onassis), Stephen Collins (JFK), Josef Sommer (Joseph Kennedy), Eve Gordon (Marilyn Monroe), Rosemary Murphy (Rose Kennedy), Joss Ackland (Aristotle Onassis), William Devane (Black Jack Bouvier), Brian Smiar (Lyndon B. Johnson), Dylan Price (Teddy Kennedy), etc. First shown on US television.

Whenever the producers of TV mini-series are in doubt as to what to film next they seem to return to Jackie Kennedy, a well-proven stand-by full of glitz, glamour and drama. Each venture into her biography gets progressively worse and *A Woman Named Jackie* is no exception. This two-parter is on a level with a comic strip in *Modern Romances* magazine. It seems hard to believe that anyone could make anything more trite and superficial, but then who knows what next season's schedules have in store for us?
The President and Mrs. Kennedy are shown arriving at Love Field. The motorcade is followed down to Dealey Plaza with an extensive use of library footage. In the Plaza a shot is heard, JFK clutches his throat (rather as if he has indigestion) and a smattering of blood appears. He then falls into Jackie's lap. A second and final shot is heard (only two shots!) but this does not appear to

hit the President. There are no signs of any head wounds but Jackie still, inexplicably in the circumstances, climbs out on to the tail of the limo. She is pushed back in and the car races to Parkland where JFK is soon declared dead. LBJ is sworn in and Air Force One takes off for Washington. Jackie takes command of the funeral arrangements (what shall I wear?) and an aide says in passing that Lee Harvey Oswald has just been shot so we'll never get to the bottom of *this* little mystery now.

[282] NIGHTLINE SPECIAL.
ABC-TV, New York. 22 November, 1991.
Color. Running time: 45 minutes approx.
Anchor: Ted Koppel. Reporter: Forrest Sawyer.

Forrest Sawyer, much to his credit, gained access to five volumes of hitherto secret KGB files on Lee Harvey Oswald held in Moscow. Further files were withheld and those that were released were santitized. Sawyer observed, 'These days you can bet that a Russian intelligence agency will not put out anything that would upset the CIA.'

Richard Snyder, the US consular officer who met Oswald at the Moscow embassy, is interviewed by Sawyer.

The program and the files are discussed in Dick Russell's *The Man Who Knew Too Much* (1992), pps201-2, 222-3.

[283] THE KENNEDYS.
Thames Television, London. 13, 20, 27 October and 3 November 1992. Producers: Phillip Whitehead, Marilyn H. Mellowes, David Espar, James A. DeVinney.
Color. Running time (total): 213 minutes.
Four part documentary first transmitted by Thames Television, London, on 13 October (*Nine Hostages to Fortune*), 20 October (*That Old Jack Magic*), 27 October (*We Are All Mortal*), and 3 November (*The Legacy*) 1992. Running times of the 4 parts are, respectively: 50, 50, 53 and 60 minutes.
Executive Producer: Roger Bolton. Writers: Geoffrey C. Ward, Phillip Whitehead, David Espar, James A. DeVinney. Historical Advisor: Alan Brinkley. Narrator: John Woodvine. Original Music: Michael Bacon. Director of Photography: John Hazard. Editors: David Espar, Richard Smigielski, Charles Scott.

Archive sources [film]: The John F. Kennedy Library, Sherman Grinberg Film Libraries, NBC News Video Archive, CBS News Film Archive, UCLA Film and Television Archive, 20th Century Fox Movietonews, Petrified Films, Library of Congress, Producers Library Service, Shields Archival, KINO International Corporation, Archive Films, National Archives and Records Administration, Franklin D. Roosevelt Library, Visnews, British Movietonews (*sic*) Film Library, Bundesarchiv, US Dept. of Defense - Norton Airforce Base, British Pathe News, WPA Film Library, Time/Life, Radharc Films, WTN Corporation.

A WGBH/Brook co-production for Thames Television, 1992.

The Kennedys is a useful if superficial documentary study of the family and its fortunes from the rise of Joe Snr. through to Ted Kennedy's aborted bid for the presidency. The value of the series is in the comprehensive selection of newsreel footage and home movies included.

Part 2, *That Old Jack Magic*, deals with the rise of JFK while Part 3, *We Are All Mortal,* is largely concerned with his presidency.

Apart from one motorcade clip there is no Dallas footage. The assassination itself is mentioned in the commentary and then after a showing of the Walter Cronkite news broadcast of the President's death the documentary hurriedly moves on to Jackie, the arrangements for the funeral and the funeral itself with only a passing reference to the Warren Commission's findings and subsequent public disquiet.

It is quite strange (if now predictable) how mainstream and academic studies of JFK shrink from confronting the assassination and the reasons behind it, shunning it as though it is not a legitimate area of inquiry. How are we to understand the life and times of a man if we do not know the reasons for his death?

Interviews of interest to the critical community are with Judith Campbell Exner, Richard Bissell, and Priscilla (Johnson) McMillan who worked as a re-searcher for JFK when he was a senator in 1953 and who would later write *Marina and Lee* (1977).

A further note on:

[232] DALLAS BELLES [aka MODERN MOTEL].
Since writing the entry above for No. 232 some further information has come to light.

On 10 June 1963 Jack Ruby made a 16-minute phone call to Candy Barr who was then living in Edna, Texas. She had been paroled from the Texas State Prison in April after serving time since 1959 on a marijuana possession conviction. In the preceeding weeks Ruby had made five calls to her and also travelled out to see her. Seth Kantor implies in his study of Ruby that he was not so much interested in Candy as gaining access through her to her boyfriend, Mickey Cohen, the Mafia chief of the West Coast, possibly for a loan in order to escape his tax difficulties. This seems unlikely as Ruby had plenty of other Mob connections nearer home for a loan. Ruby called Candy again, on 12 November, and spoke to her for 14 minutes.

A number of questions arise from these facts. How well did Ruby know

Candy? Did she ever strip for him at the Carousel? Ruby was in Dallas when *Smart Aleck* was made. Knowing the Mob's interest in pornography as a business we can legitimately ask whether there was Mob involvement in the production and distribution of *Smart Aleck* and whether Ruby himself had a hand in it?

Candy Barr was interviewed in *Oui* magazine in June 1976, though she was not asked about Ruby or the background to the film. She lives in New York now with another woman. Somebody from the critical community should contact her.

Seth Kantor's references are on pps21-3 of his *Who Was Jack Ruby?* (1978).

Appendix: Titles by Chapter and Year of Issue

References are to entry numbers not page numbers.

1: LEE HARVEY OSWALD IN NEW ORLEANS

   1963

2: DEALEY PLAZA

   22 November 1963

3: PARKLAND, LOVE FIELD, DALLAS POST-ASSASSINATION

22 November 1963 onwards

4: TV BROADCASTS: 22 NOVEMBER 1963 AND AFTER

22-25 November 1963

5: DOCUMENTARY FILMS, TV PROGRAMS, VIDEOS

1963

1964

8: THEATRICAL MOTION PICTURES

9: LOST, UNCONFIRMED, SPURIOUS, UNREALIZED, AND FORTHCOMING FILMS

10: NORTH AMERICAN FILM, TV, AND NEWSREEL LIBRARIES WITH ASSASSINATION FOOTAGE

References

Frequent reference is made in the preceeding chapters to *The Third Decade* (subtitled *A Journal of Research on the John F. Kennedy Assassination*). This is a bi-monthly edited and published by Jerry D. Rose from State University College, Fredonia, New York 14063, USA. This is essential reading for any serious critic of the assassination.

Information on the feature films above has largely come from *Variety* (Los Angeles), *The New York Times, Screen International* (London) and the *Monthly Film Bulletin* (London, the British Film Institute). Readers requiring further information and fuller credit listings are directed to these sources. The *New York Times* film reviews have, fortunately, been gathered, published and indexed in six magnificent volumes: *The New York Times Film Reviews 1913-1968,* New York: The NY Times and Arno Press, 1980. Supplements have also been published. Not to be outdone *Variety* did the same thing, and in 16 volumes, no less: *Variety Film Reviews 1907-1980,* Hollywood-New York-London: Film Archive and Garland Publishing, 1983.

What follows here is a list of the more reliable and better researched volumes known to me on the JFK assassination that I found useful in producing the present work together with other works mentioned in the text. It is by no means exhaustive.

I have not bothered to list official government reports and such here. Guth and Wrone detail those published up until 1979, and this may be supplemented by the useful bibliography in Scheim's *Contract on America* (1988), pps462-5, that casts the net wider to include reports from organised crime hearings.

American Heritage Magazine. See United Press International.
Anson, Robert Sam. *"They've Killed the President!" The Search for the Murderers of John F. Kennedy.* New York: Bantam Books, 1975.

Blakey, G. Robert, and Billings, Richard. *The Plot to Kill the President: Organized Crime Assassinated JFK.* New York: Times Books, 1981.

Bliss, Michael. *Brian De Palma.* Metuchen, New Jersey: Scarecrow Press, 1983.

Blumenthal, Sid, and Yazijian, Harvey. *Government by Gunplay: Assassination Conspiracy Theories from Dallas to Today.* New York: Signet/New American Library, 1976.

Buchanan, Thomas G. *Who Killed Kennedy?* New York: Putnam, 1964. London: Secker & Warburg, 1964.

Condon, Richard. *Winter Kills.* New York: Dial Press, 1974.

Crenshaw, M.D., Charles A., with Hansen, Jens, and Shaw, J. Gary. *JFK: Conspiracy of Silence.* New York: Signet/Penguin, 1992.

Craig, Roger. *When They Kill a President.* Reprinted, Dallas: JFK Assassination Information Center, 1992.

Crow, Duncan. *World in Action.* London: Mayflower/Dell, 1965.

Davis, John. *Mafia Kingfish: Carlos Marcello and The Assassination of John F. Kennedy.* New York: McGraw-Hill, 1988.

De Witt, Judith. *The Kennedys.* London: Screen Guides/Thames Television, 1992. [A 'souvenir' to accompany No. 283.]

DiEugenio, James. *Destiny Betrayed: JFK, Cuba, and the Garrison Case.* New York: Sheridan Square Press, 1992.

Di Lauro, Al, and Rabkin, Gerald. *Dirty Movies: An Illustrated History of the Stag Film 1915-1970.* New York: Chelsea House, 1976.

Duffy, James R. *The Web: Kennedy Assassination Cover-Up.* Gloucester, England: Alan Sutton Publishing, 1988. US edition as *Who Killed JFK? The Kennedy Assassination Cover-Up.* New York: Shapolsky Publishers, 1989.

Eddowes, Michael. *The Oswald File.* New York: Clarkson N. Potter, 1977.

Eddowes, Michael. *Lee Harvey Oswald: Report on the Activities of an Impostor who Assassinated President John F. Kennedy.* [London]: Self-published, 1978.

Eddowes, Michael. *Kruschev Killed Kennedy.* [Dallas?]: Self published, [1978?].

Epstein, Edward J. *Legend: The Secret World of Lee Harvey Oswald.* New York: Reader's Digest Press/McGraw Hill, 1978. London: Arrow Books, 1978.

Epstein, Edward J. *The Assassination Chronicles: Inquest, Counterplot, and Legend.* New York: Carroll and Graf, 1992.

Flammonde, Paris. *The Kennedy Conspiracy: An Uncommissioned Report on the Jim Garrison Investigation.* New York: Meredith, 1969.

Freed, Donald, and Lane, Mark. *Executive Action: Assassination of a Head of State.* Introduction by Richard H. Popkin. New York: Dell, 1973. London: Charisma Books, 1973.

Frewin, Anthony. *Late-Breaking News on Clay Shaw's United Kingdom Contacts*. Dallas: The JFK Assassination Information Center, 1992.

Garrison, Jim. *A Heritage of Stone*. New York: Putnam, 1970.

Garrison, Jim. *On the Trail of the Assassins: My Investigation and Prosecution of the Murder of President Kennedy*. New York: Sheridan Square Press, 1988. London: Penguin Books, 1992.

Groden, Robert. 'The JFK Assassination: A New Look at the Zapruder Film' in *Rolling Stone* (New York), April 1975.

Groden, Robert, and Model, Peter. *JFK: The Case for Conspiracy*. New York: Manor Books, 1976.

Groden, Robert. 'The JFK Assassination Evidence That Nobody Wanted to Reveal' in *Argosy* (New York), August 1977.

Groden, Robert, and Livingstone, Harrison E. *High Treason: The Assassination of President John F. Kennedy - What Really Happened*. Boothwyn, Pa.: The Conservatory Press, 1989 (all references herein to this edition). New York, Berkley Books, 1990.

Guth, DeLloyd J., and Wrone, David R. *The Assassination of John F. Kennedy: A Comprehensive Historical and Legal Bibliography, 1963-1979*. Westport, Connecticut: Greenwood Press, 1980.

Hamilton, Nigel. *JFK: Life and Death of an American President*. Volume One: *Reckless Youth*. New York: Random House, 1992.

Hasford, Gustav. *The Short-Timers*. New York: Harper & Row, 1979.

Hepburn, James. *Farewell America*. Vaduz (Liechtenstein): Frontiers, 1968.

Hinckle, Warren, and Turner, William. *Deadly Secrets: The CIA Mafia War Against Castro and the Assassination of JFK*. New York: Thunder's Mouth Press, 1992 (originally published as *The Fish is Red*, New York: Harper & Row, 1981).

Hurt, Henry. *Reasonable Doubt: An Investigation into the Assassination of John F. Kennedy*. New York: Holt, Rinehart and Winston, 1986.

Itek Corporation. *John Kennedy Film Analysis*. Lexington, Mass.: Itek Corporation, 1976.

Joesten, Joachim. *The Garrison Enquiry: Truth and Consequences*. London: Peter Dawnay, 1967.

Kantor, Seth. *Who Was Jack Ruby?* New York: Everest House, 1978.

Kirkwood, James. *American Grotesque: An Account of the Clay Shaw-Jim Garrison Affair in the City of New Orleans*. New York: Simon and Schuster, 1970.

Kubrick, Stanley, Herr, Michael, and Hasford, Gustav. *Full Metal Jacket: The Screenplay*. New York: Alfred A. Knopf/Borzoi, 1987.

Kurtz, Michael L. *Crime of the Century: The Kennedy Assassination from A Historian's Perspective*. Knoxville, Tennessee: University of Tennessee Press, 1982.

La Fountaine, George. *Flashpoint*. New York: Fawcett, 1984.

Lane, Mark. *Rush to Judgement: A Critique of the Warren Commission's Inquiry into the Murder of President John F. Kennedy, Officer J. D. Tippit, and Lee Harvey Oswald.* Introduction by Hugh Trevor-Roper. New York: Holt, Rinehart and Winston, 1966.

Lane, Mark. *A Citizen's Dissent: Mark Lane Replies.* New York: Holt, Rinehart and Winston, 1968. New York: Fawcett Crest, 1969.

Lane, Mark. *Plausible Denial: Was the CIA Involved in the Assassination of JFK?* New York: Thunder's Mouth Press, 1991.

Lifton, David. *Best Evidence: Disguise and Deception in the Assassination of John F. Kennedy.* New York and London: Macmillan Publishing/Collier Macmillan Publishers, 1980. Third edition: with 7 autopsy photographs and 'Epilogue to 1982 Edition' and an 'Afterword' - New York: Carroll and Graf, 1988.

Livingstone, Harrison E. *High Treason 2: The Great Cover-Up: The Assassination of President John F. Kennedy.* New York: Carroll & Graf, 1992.

Manchester, William. *The Death of a President: November 20-November 25, 1963.* New York: Harper & Row, 1967. London: Michael Joseph, 1967.

Martin, David C. *Wilderness of Mirrors.* New York: Harper and Row, 1980.

Marrs, Jim. *Crossfire: The Plot That Killed Kennedy.* New York: Carroll & Graf, 1989.

McMillan, Priscilla Johnson. *Marina and Lee.* New York: Harper & Row, 1977. London: Collins, 1978.

Meagher, Sylvia. *Accessories After the Fact: The Warren Commission, the Authorities, and the Report.* Introduction by Leo Sauvage. Indianapolis: Bobbs-Merrill, 1967. New York: Vintage Books, 1976. Preface by Senator Richard S. Schweiker. Introduction by Peter Dale Scott.

Meagher, Sylvia, and Owens, Gary. *Master Index to the JFK Assassination Investigations.* Metuchen, New Jersey: Scarecrow Press, 1966.

Menninger, Bonar. *Mortal Error: The Shot That Killed JFK.* New York: St Martin's Press, 1992. London: Sidgwick & Jackson, 1992.

North, Mark. *Act of Treason: The Role of J. Edgar Hoover in the Assassination of President Kennedy.* New York: Carroll and Graf, 1991.

Oglesby, Carl. *The JFK Assassination: The Facts and the Theories.* Afterword by Norman Mailer. New York: Signet/Penguin, 1992.

Ostrovsky, Victor, and Hoy, Claire. *By Way of Deception.* New York: St Martin's Press, 1990.

Pell, Derek. *Assassination Rhapsody.* New York: Autonomedia/Semiotext(e) Foreign Agents Series, 1989.

Prouty, L. Fletcher. *JFK: The CIA, Vietnam, and the Plot to Assassinate John F. Kennedy.* New York: Birch Lane Press/Carol Publishing Group.

Russell, Dick. *The Man Who Knew Too Much.* New York: Carroll & Graf / Richard Gallen, 1992. Foreword by Carl Oglesby.

Sahl, Mort. *Heartland.* New York: Harcourt Brace, 1976.

Scally, Christopher. *'So Near...and Yet So Far': The House Select Committee on Assassinations' Investigation into the Murder of President John F. Kennedy.* [Dallas: JFK Assassination Information Center, 1990 (?)].

Scheim, David E. *Contract on America: The Mafia Murder of President John F. Kennedy.* New York: Shapolsky Publishers, 1988.

Scott, Peter Dale, Hoch, Paul L., and Stetler, Russell. *The Assassinations: Dallas and Beyond: A Guide to Cover-ups and Investigations.* New York: Random House, 1976. Abridged and revised edition: Harmondsworth (Middlesex): Pelican Books, 1978.

Shapiro, Stanley. *A Time to Remember.* New York: Random House, 1986.

Singer, Loren. *The Parallax View.* Garden City, New York: Doubleday, 1970.

Smith, Matthew. *JFK: The Second Plot.* Edinburgh: Mainstream Publishing, 1992.

Sprague, Richard E. 'The Assassination of President Kennedy: The Application of Computers to the Photographic Evidence' in *Computers and Automation* (Washington DC), May/July 1970.

Stone, Oliver, and Sklar, Zachary. *JFK - The Book of the Film: The Documentary Screenplay.* Research notes by Jane Rusconi. New York: Applause Books, 1992.

Summers, Anthony. *Conspiracy.* New York: McGraw-Hill, 1981. London: Collins, 1981. Revised edition as *The Kennedy Conspiracy.* London: Sphere Books, 1989.

Thompson, Josiah. *Six Seconds in Dallas: A Micro-Study of the Kennedy Assassination.* New York: Bernard Geis Associates, 1967.

United Press International, with American Heritage Magazine. *Four Days: The Historical Record of the Death of President Kennedy.* [New York]: American Heritage, 1964.

Weisberg, Harold. *Whitewash II: The FBI-Secret Service CoverUp.* Hyattstown, Maryland: the author, 1966. New York: Dell, 1967.

Weisberg, Harold. *Photographic Whitewash: Suppressed Kennedy Assassina tion Pictures.* Hyattstown, Maryland: the author, 1967, 1976.

Weisberg, Harold. *Oswald in New Orleans: Case of Conspiracy with the C.I.A.* New York: Canyon Books, 1967.

White, Stephen. *Should We Now Believe the Warren Report?* Preface by Walter Cronkite. New York: The Macmillan Company/London: Collier-Macmillan, 1968.

Index of Interviews and Witnesses

References are to entry numbers not page numbers.

Interviewers, reporters, presenters and similar are not included in this index. For instance, Mark Lane appears here when he is being interviewed but not when he is doing the interviewing.

Most major documentaries and investigations contain footage of Lee Harvey Oswald and Jack Ruby. Here I have indexed only a few of the more noteworthy clips.

Index of Entry Titles

Chapters 10 and 11 have not been indexed here.

Index of TV Stations and Production Companies

Index of Presenters,
Reporters, and Narrators

Truth never envelops itself in
mystery; and the mystery in
which it is at any time
enveloped is the work
of its antagonist,
and never of
itself.

- Thomas Paine (1794)

About the Compiler

ANTHONY FREWIN is an assistant director for Warner Bros. in Europe. He is an associate of the JFK Assassination Information Center in Dallas, Texas, and has long studied and researched materials describing it. His latest book is *Late-Breaking News on Clay Shaw's United Kingdom Contacts* (1992).

www.ingramcontent.com/pod-product-compliance
Lightning Source LLC
Chambersburg PA
CBHW070444100426
42812CB00004B/1204